WHAT
Handwriting
TELLS YOU

WHAT *Handwriting*

TELLS YOU *about yourself,*

your friends and famous people

A PIONEER WORK ON GRAPHOANALYSIS

by **M. N. BUNKER**

Nelson-Hall nh Chicago

ISBN 911012-02-8

CONTENTS

INTRODUCTION

This book was written and first published more than a quarter of a century ago. It was an important volume then and it still is important today, but for somewhat different reasons.

In 1939 M. N. Bunker completed formulating the basic principles and theories upon which Graphoanalysis is based. Much work was yet to be done, but as an appeal for public awareness of the promising new developments, *What Handwriting Tells You* was written almost immediately.

This is a pioneering work that attempted to explain in a popular fashion the valuable new techniques used to identify character and personality from handwriting.

You should be aware while reading this book that today's techniques of Graphoanalysis are far more advanced and sophisticated than those presented in these pages. New developments in science in general, and in human understanding, particularly, have been achieved at a revolutionary rate since 1939.

Changes in Graphoanalysis have occurred at an equally astonishing pace until now this new technique has taken its place alongside other accepted psychological testing methods as a sound and complex tool for personality assessment.

Nevertheless, the basic principles and findings of Mr. Bunker remain applicable today to the teachings of Graphoanalysis. This book, then, is important because it contains those principles still basically correct—although presented here in a simplified form. Secondly, the volume is historically important and interesting.

This primer of Graphoanalysis should not be considered a course. Professional courses in scientific handwriting analysis, frankly, are not "easy." A General Course in Graphoanalysis taught by the International Graphoanalysis Society of Chicago takes about a year and a half to complete.

The taste of handwriting analysis given on these pages does not (and cannot) include what is considered the heart of Graphoanalysis: evaluation.

In fact, it is evaluation that distinguishes scientific Graphoanalysis from the many occult interpretations of handwriting, all of which are called graphology. It has been said that Graphoanalysis is to graphology as astronomy is to astrology.

In scientific handwriting analysis there is no simple one-for-one relationship between a graphic sign on paper and a trait of personality. Identifying a trait of character is a complex procedure. The Graphoanalyst must be conscious of and he must consider a whole constellation of variables. To keep using the one-for-one "principles" is a complete denial of the almost universally accepted belief in the importance of inter-relating personality traits.

Despite its obvious imperfections and limitations, *What Handwriting Tells You* is being reprinted without revisions. It is the first book on Graphoanalysis, written in the very early days of this psychological technique, and it was written by the founder of Graphoanalysis, M. N. Bunker. These two reasons alone make the book important—which is quite apart from the steady demand there is for this most interesting work on Graphoanalysis.

V. Peter Ferrara, President
International Graphoanalysis Society
Chicago, Illinois U.S.A.

June 1965

CHAPTER I

HOW GRAPHO-ANALYSIS GOT ITS START

Kings and queens of the movie world, barons of finance, social climbers as well as those already arrived in the social world, authors, artists, dancers, and men and women from every known profession and walk of life, women of the streets and wolves of the bowery, leaders in business and politics and the famous of the earth have asked me to read their handwriting. They have all come for grapho-analyses, and then have sent their friends. My study walls are lined with their signed photographs, and my filing cabinets are filled with their letters of comment and appreciation, but there is not one single copy of an analysis that has been made. Very early in my professional life I made a rule that has not been broken. Once a handwriting specimen had been analyzed, there was nothing to reveal what that analysis had said; no copies, no notes. If necessary, a new analysis could be made, but there have been no carbon copies of the secrets that so many times might have ruined lives if published.

So grapho-analysis has brought me friends, and these friends have very often asked questions that showed keen interest in the history of handwriting analysis. "How did you come to start it?" "Where did you learn it?" and other questions, which, if answered individually, would have taken almost all of my working hours. However, they have been honest questions and deserve an honest answer.

Picture for yourself, if you will, miles of closely-curled buffalo grass, burning gray brown under a blazing sun, and broken here and there by ripening wheat. Cattle. Long days under the open sky, keeping the shifting herds together. That was my country and those were my days. Stretched on the springy mattress of the growing grass, I read my first book on graphology. The low-walled ranch house had the remnants of a well-chosen library—Milton, Dickens, Shakespeare. I read all of them along with chance magazines. I read the advertisements in those magazines, answered them, then read the literature that came in reply to my requests. One of these advertisements offered a sixteen-page book on graphology that attracted my attention, and laid the groundwork for more reading about graphology, finally leading to serious study of how writing could be analyzed, and also why graphology had so many apparent contradictions.

Long before that, however, I had been drilled in the idea that sometime I would become an expert pen artist and would have employment in Washington, where I would have an assignment engrossing government documents. It was in the days when even postmasters' appoint-ments were prepared by an expert penman, and important government papers were engrossed. The future looked promising. Night after night after I had brought in the herd, I sat at the old kitchen table, doing ovals, practicing letter formations. A short session spent in the old York Business College in eastern Nebraska, under the guidance of Prof. A. B. Opfer, had increased my determination to become a great penman. Mr. Opfer talked me into parting with a hard-earned half dollar for a year's subscription to the old *Western Penman,* where I found a series of lessons prepared by S. C. Bedinger, for many years a member of the faculty of the Oklahoma Agricultural and Mechanical College. I liked the Bedinger writing but am not quite sure, even to this day, whether it was his style of penman-ship or the necktie he wore in the picture heading his lesson page that kept me working on the various exercises.

However, in spite of all the practice of the various drills, I was having trouble. My handwriting simply would not adjust itself to the styles in the magazines, so, after months of effort, I submitted a page of my work to the very famous Prof. A. W. Dakin, whose studio was the gathering point of some of the greatest penmen of that generation. Mr. Dakin criticized my work, giving me a world of encouragement by saying I could become a great penman if I would do just one thing to my writing.

Mr. Dakin wanted me to cut the tails off my words. That is, he wanted me to make my writing more compact, and leave off the long finishing strokes.

Those two requirements he considered necessary, and it was those two simple but necessary improvements that actually started me on the road to becoming a grapho-analyst. I tried to take the Dakin prescription straight and found that I could not write the way he instructed. I had to put finishes or long final strokes on my words, and I could not crowd the letters together.

Why? That was what I wanted to know. How was it that Mr. Dakin could make the most beautifully formed letters, and leave off the long finishing strokes, while I scattered my letters far apart, and put on long finishes floating out like the tail of a kite? I wondered. It was my problem, with me early and late, until I came across a beautifully flourished envelope done by C. W. Ransom whose pen-manship lessons were being advertised all over the world. Mr. Ransom's writing filled me with hope. Here was a man who did not write a compact hand, who put flourishes on his words and who had won the World's First Prize for a course of lessons in business writing.

That summer I carried the Ransomerian School letters around with me while I herded the cattle. I wanted that course but did not have the money. It seemed utterly use-less to think about it, but finally, as the winter came on,

Mr. Ransom made arrangements so that I might study with him by mail, without paying, and thereby demonstrated the meaning of those long finals in his own writing as well as mine. He did not know the value of a dollar. I wanted to study his lessons and could not afford to pay for them, so he let me have them, believing that somehow or another, in the long run, he would be paid.

I did not know this then, but during the years of research that followed, those widely separated letters and long finals have proved themselves as accurate evidence of a nature that lacks money sense. Such a writer may make money, but he will give it just as freely, because he does not have the trait of accumulating, that so many men and women consider necessary. Mr. Ransom made long finals, indeed they may have been too long, and there may have been too many of them, but he was a great man and a great teacher. Mr. Dakin was right and Mr. Ransom was right. They were both right, because each wrote as he lived. Each had a vital part in feeding the necessary *why* that drove me further and further into the field of handwriting investigation.

My first articles on handwriting were published by the old *Spencerian Magazine* in 1911. That magazine, devoted largely to Spencerian shorthand, was edited by Professor Spencer, whose shorthand system I had studied. When I sent him an article on the value of good handwriting in business he accepted it. He ordered another, and in the December, 1910 issue sealed my fate by editorially announcing my articles under the heading, *The Pen is Mightier* and by calling me an expert. After that sort of introduction, I had to go ahead.

Teachers of handwriting generally were saying that "there wasn't anything to graphology," and the graphologists were taking specimens provided by those teachers and their pupils and analyzing them with sufficient accuracy to justify their laughing at the professional penmen. However, the graphologists were making mistakes too; often enough to make the laughter embarrassing when the teachers laughed. In short, the graphologists missed and they hit, so that I found myself facing another *why*.

Both teachers and graphologists dealt in strokes, but like the man who could not see the forest for the trees, they missed the big truth. They were each looking at letters, and not at the combination of strokes out of which letters were made. This principle answers the question that has been asked so many times, "If I write differently at different times, how can you tell anything about me?"

Your pen strokes are the foundation on which your analysis is made. If you write backhand once, and forward at another time, you will still put into your pen strokes truths which will provide a complete picture of you.

With the discovery of this stroke principle it was easy to understand why the graphologists had missed. They were saying that if an *o* was made open-mouthed, it represented a frank or talkative nature. They were right, but what if they did not have an *o* to give them this information? Would they have still been able to get at the truth about a writer?

It seemed natural to me to look at the open *o* as expressing a mental habit, so that if such an *o* meant frankness, a circle stroke made in a similar way should give the same facts even though the *o* itself were missing. If an open *o* meant frankness, then it was open, and any circle open at the top would mean openness or frankness.

All of this, however, took years to determine, and my only start in graphology had been a little sixteen-page booklet with just fifteen specimen lines of writing, and fifteen rules.

That little book, though, was a reflection of another book written more than three hundred years before by a scholar in Southern Europe whose *Treating of How a Written Message May Reveal the Nature and Qualities of the Writer* was the first bound book on the subject. More than sixteen hundred years before this book was published by Camillo Baldo, the Emperor Nero pointed out a certain man at court and said, "His writing shows him to be treacherous."

Long before I spent my dollar for Professor Hausam's little brown pamphlet, graphology had contributed in one way or another to the findings of criminologists, psychiatrists, and other researchers. Goethe in Germany had been a student of graphology. Robert and Elizabeth Browning had spent time mastering the rules of handwriting analysis available to them. In America the erratic genius of Edgar Allan Poe had been attracted to the subject to the extent that he had written a book on it.

Even the author of *The Scarlet Letter* recognized the existence of handwriting analysis, although when Hawthorne wrote in his essay, "There are said to be temperaments endowed with sympathies so exquisite that, by merely handling an autograph they can detect the writer's character with unerring accuracy, and read his inmost heart as easily as a less gifted eye would peruse the written page," he showed utter lack of knowledge of the subject. Grapho-analysis does not involve the occult. Instead, handwriting is a splendid example of cause and effect with laws that do not change.

It did not take me long to work this out, but it did take years of testing and retesting to discover the answer to the *why* which troubled me while I lay on my back under the desert sun and watched my herd of cattle.

It took the examination of countless specimens of writing, which fortunately came to me during my years of editorial work, teaching, and association with people of all classes. Those writers were a testing laboratory where each explanation could be checked and counterchecked. Thousands of those whose writing I analyzed never knew that I had read their writing, and later when we visited together, they did not know that many of my questions were asked in an effort to check my findings.

In this way I learned that one combination of pen strokes reveals a lover of sweets and rich gravies, while another combination of strokes indicates a writer who prefers simple salads to thick steaks. All of these determinations can be made, and *you* can make them if you really apply yourself to the use of the principles of grapho-analysis.

During the years, countless men and women have helped by confirming or denying my findings. Those who have studied their reports and found them precisely accurate have encouraged me, but those who have pointed out defects have done even more to make possible the precise principles which you will find in the following pages.

These men and women are all part of the history of grapho-analysis, and they deserve credit for their part in the years of research that has won for the science warm praise from such an expert as the late A. P. Meub, who had been a member of the teaching staff of the Woodrow Wilson High School, Pasadena, California.

Mr. Meub was one of America's ablest penmen. He taught thousands of young men and women to write, and advised many of them to have their handwriting analyzed. All of this helped in the progress of graphoanalysis, but more important was the fact that Mr. Meub represented that group of fine penmen who forty years ago were saying, "It cannot be done." They were talking about graphology as they knew it then and they were telling at least something of the truth.

This, after all, is the thing that justifies the position that grapho-analysis is not graphology, and that the break I made when I discovered the answer to my first *why* about the tails on the end of my words was justified. Grapho-analysis is not graphology, but it would not be here today if it had not been for Camillo Baldo, the Italian scholar, or Abbe Michon who took up Baldo's efforts and made them known.

Graphology considers letter formations primarily, while grapho-analysis considers stroke values first, and then relatively, or the effect of one stroke upon another. Each individual stroke, perpendicular or horizontal, each hook, whether large or small, and each loop whether above or below the line, has an individual value which is primary, but each of these individual values may be affected by other values found in every specimen of handwriting. Because this is true, a page of miscellaneous pen strokes is

885 N. Holliston Ave.,
Pasadena, Calif.

Dear Dr. Bunker:

The analysis of my handwriting has been received, and I hasten to tell you that you have hit me to a T. The reading is really remarkable, and I wonder at your accuracy. You are the master.

I think of all the good you can do in helping people, especially youth, find themselves. You can depend on me to recommend your service.

Sincerely,

Albert P. Newb.

sufficient for a long analysis of any character. The value of the handwriting in a page is in the wide variation of strokes, curves, curls, and hooks provided by a page as against the absence of such variations in a page made up of nothing but disconnected strokes.

Now you know the story of grapho-analysis and you are ready to take up a group of new rules that will keep you busy testing and proving their accuracy. They are simple rules, but some of them are very revealing. You will learn a great many intimate details about people whom you think you know, and some of them are almost certain to astonish you.

You may think you have accomplished a feat of magic but you have not. If you learn these rules and apply them properly you will get the truth.

CHAPTER II

YOU TOO CAN ANALYZE HANDWRITING SUCCESSFULLY

You can learn to analyze handwriting. You can do it easily, and at the same time enjoy every step of the way, because the more you learn the more you will want to learn. Mastering grapho-analysis is very much like playing a fascinating game. Each new handwriting is an interesting experience, where you test your skill and astonish yourself by your own accuracy.

You can become so skillful that you can take the writing of a stranger whom you have never seen and about whom you know absolutely nothing, and draw a clear, accurate word picture of the writer's character, personality and ability. You can do such an amazing piece of work that you will startle those who see you make the analysis and who will, in turn, tell their friends about your ability. Almost at once you will find yourself the center of interest with people asking to meet you. Wherever you go, you will be the subject of interested conversation among those whom you meet, with so many friends that you will forget any feeling you may have had of being a wall-flower.

All of this is possible not six months or a year from now, but shortly. There are thirteen chapters following this one. In each of these divisions you will find easy instruction and examples so that if you devote thirty minutes a day to reading these rules, and then test them out on your friends, you will find at the end of a single month that you have gained knowledge and skill that you will be loath to part with for any sum. You will have increased your own happiness immeasurably; you will have found new interests and have gained an understanding of people that you may never have thought possible.

All of this may seem impossible now, but after a few months you will find that instead of having been too optimistic about what you can do, you may have greatly underestimated your possibilities. You will discover at the end of even a month of reading and testing that you have learned things that will save you money, keep you out of trouble, and even give you a chance to earn money by learning how to deal with people. All of this in addition to adding to your personal popularity.

These promises are being made to you personally, on the basis of what men and women whom I have never seen, but who have studied with me just as you are studying with me, have told me of their experiences. Take this letter from one of my students, whose handwriting won a prize in a contest for the "most unusual handwriting" submitted. The writer is a wife and mother, living in a small South Carolina town. "One of the chief benefits of my study," she writes, "has been its service in bridging the chasm of strangeness that often lies between new acquaintances. I do not mean that grapho-analysis is merely a good ice-breaker—though it serves amazingly well when it is necessary. It means more than that, for when I can offer a person an understanding of his personality, I immediately gain his appreciation and confidence, and the friendship is accelerated."

This woman has put the simple rules of grapho-analysis to a test, so that she knows what she is talking about, and she is not alone. There are hundreds of others—men and women from all corners of the world, who have studied grapho-analysis rules, and who say the same thing. It is on their word and their experiences, that these promises of your increased personal popularity and general improvement are made to you.

You may be very busy, and you may be more interested in getting a job and filling it than in gaining popularity. If so, here is another lady who studied these rules and who tells her own story from her home in Auckland, New Zealand. She studied the same rules you will find in the following chapters. She put them to the same tests to which you can put them in your own home, and among your own friends, so that she did not have advantages that you do not have.

"It has helped me know my fellow men," she says. "It has brought me in contact with important people. One evening, soon after my arrival in New Zealand from Canada, I was introduced to the manager of one of the largest fruit exporting firms in the country. To my amazement the party who made the introduction added, 'Yes, and she can analyze handwriting. She read mine very well, and I know it was right, for I'm a bit of an expert at it myself.' This gentleman to whom I was introduced became very much interested in what I told him about himself from his handwriting, so called my bluff. He withdrew from his pocket an envelope, and asked me about the writer. I told him exactly what I found in the writing. As a result of this chance meeting, I started to work the next morning for this gentleman's firm, and I must say I am being given every opportunity for advancement. They have an office staff of over three hundred employees, and I am being given special consideration because I can analyze handwriting. I met my employer because I could take his handwriting and tell him about himself, because I could take the writing of friends of his, about whom I knew nothing, and tell him the truth about them. I secured my present position because of this knowledge, all of which was made possible by using my spare moments, learning rules that anyone can learn. It was a lot of fun to learn, but now my knowledge has proved its value in a strange land."

Of course you may be so busy in your present position that you do not want to learn anything more to increase your value, either to yourself or to your employer. There may be men and women who are so self-satisfied that they do not want to improve their earning ability, but even if this is true, there is still another benefit to be gained by following out the principles set forth in the following chapters. This is simple neighborliness or the ability to understand the folks among whom you live, and to get along with them. It is in such circumstances that the rules of handwriting analysis have a value that cannot be estimated in words. One student who studied with me a long time ago, puts it this way:

"We must cultivate neighborliness. Grapho-analysis enables us more fully to understand and appreciate our neighbors." There is good in every one if we only look for it, and we can find the truth about that good in his handwriting. Strategy in handling people can be developed and strengthened by learning the simple rules of grapho-analysis. Our success financially depends upon how well we can handle people. Others can make or break us by their good or ill will, and when we can take a stranger's handwriting and learn that he is warmhearted and kindly, even if he does act hard-boiled, we have an advantage that others who can see only the outer man, do not have. On the other hand, some of the meanest and most cruel men and women in the world have charming outside manners and, if we depend only on what we can see, we are certain to make serious mistakes. If, on the other hand, we can read their pen strokes, even in their poorest writing, we are able to set up a guard that can be extremely valuable.

These others, men and women in ordinary walks of life, have said these things after they have learned and tested the rules which you will find as you go ahead with your reading. Of course, there is one thing that is very important, and which you cannot afford to overlook. These men and women did not merely read the rules and then lay them aside. They read them, then dug out old letters from friends, and tested each of the rules as applied to the writing of persons they knew. They tested and proved the rules as they went along.

When they found the rule that explained stubbornness, they kept it in mind, and then watched for this sign in the handwriting of their friends and of strangers. When they found the rule regarding sensitiveness, they checked up in the writing of their friends, finding how many were sensitive. In this way they learned the truth of these rules by actually putting them to use. You will find it an interesting thing to do, because when you have applied one rule and found that it is true, you will naturally be eager to take another rule and see for yourself that it is workable.

The chances are that you have plenty of old letters in desks, old trunks or the attic. Also you know your friends and relatives, how they act, and what they say. Their letters give you plenty of material on which to practice each of the new principles as you come to them.

You may keep your new study a secret, or if you wish, you may interest your friends whom you will find eager to help you by submitting samples of their own and others' handwriting. After you have learned only a few rules, you can seem to perform wonders with your knowledge, so that if you let your friends in on the tests you are making, you will find their approval adds spice to the game.

On the other hand, if you prefer to hide your light under a bushel, you will be able to get many handwriting specimens that otherwise might not be submitted to you. In this quiet search, you will run on to some amazing things about people which, after you have found them in the handwriting, will reveal themselves in the writers' personal lives.

One thing you can absolutely count upon. The rules by which you read or analyze handwriting are not difficult, but they are exact. Almost thirty years ago when I was first fascinated by the idea of taking a page of strange handwriting and learning all about the writer, the "learning how" was much different from what you will find it in this book. I had few rules to guide me and even those that did exist were uncertain, so that, like a man walking a slippery path, I never knew when I would make a serious mistake. You do not have to face such difficulties. Your rules are fully illustrated with examples, so that every step will be clear and certain, very much unlike the old days, which you read about in Chapter One.

Possibly the most striking of all your first experiences will be the eagerness with which people listen to you and help you in every way that they can. Mr. Clark Irvine, famous newspaper man and health lecturer, enjoyed his own experiences so much that in his book *Health* he advised men and women everywhere to study handwriting analysis.

"Improve your handwriting. This personality billboard reveals much to the expert, even the amateur eye. Read a book on this subject; it is interesting, educational, and will enlighten you. Besides, it's lots of fun to be an oracle when out in company. One may have heaps of good fun in analyzing guests and friends, and it is quite simple to learn. I often use it socially, and in business it has always proved of great value in giving me a clue to the inner personality of the person with whom I am about to do business. Also, in a personal way it is of inestimable value.

Once when crossing the Pacific I had a barrel of fun giving brief analyses to my fellow passengers by merely glancing at their handwriting."

In my own experience wherever I have gone, there have been eager questioners who have asked over and over again, "Tell me what you find." They have listened eagerly, hopefully, even when they have found that their handwriting reveals traits which they have always considered very bad. They have been earnest, attentive, and will be so to you, too, so that you will sometimes wonder how you missed the joys of handwriting revelation for so long. You will find yourself attracting and holding new friends, who will overwhelm you with their gratitude for the help you have given them.

Tom Keene, the movie actor and author, puts the situation rather well in his letter. His friends told him about grapho-analysis, so he wrote asking for a personal report. His letter gives a splendid portrait of the actor. He is utterly self-reliant; even as a small boy he was self-reliant, stood on his own feet, took his punishment if he had any coming, and as he grew older, this trait grew stronger. Furthermore, as he met obstacles, his will to overcome them grew in proportion to the difficulty he met. He is positive in all of his ideas. If he says "no" he means exactly what he says. This writing shows that he is neither a deceiver nor a liar, and that he is capable of making decisions and standing by them. He possesses an almost unlimited amount of enduring determination. The undertaking that he has at hand, or the plans he may have for the future may all go askew, but if Tom Keene has once set his mind to go through with it, he will do it. His determination shows this. His brain works rapidly so that

he learns easily, and as he learns, he asks himself *Why?* almost constantly. This means that he weighs the things he learns. He finds out if they are true. This short letter reveals a highly developed sense of musical appreciation. It does not reveal that Tom Keene plays a musical instrument, but it does show that he catches the feel of music and that he understands the spirit of music and enjoys it. There are many other truths revealed in this short letter, each of which has its own part in completing the detailed and accurate picture of Tom Keene as he lives and breathes day after day.

There are two traits, though, that stand out more clearly than any other. One is his pride, which is so highly developed that he will not stoop to do anything small or petty at any time. It is a quality of personal integrity that keeps him above the cheap or tawdry things of life. The other is his highly developed sense of selection when it comes to intimate friends. As a small boy Tom Keene had only one or two close chums; as he grew older, he met many people, appreciated their good qualities, as they appreciated his, but he still has only one or two intimate chums.

How do I know this? Well, here is a little secret, revealed by the first rule that you have among all of them. It always holds good. When you find a writer who makes a little square box at the finish of his *y*, or *g* as Tom Keene does in this letter, you have a writer who is clannish in the selection of friends or business associates. Such a writer may know a great many people, may be a good mixer, but underneath there is a distinct orthodoxy in the selection of close friends. Tom Keene's writing shows it, and you may be surprised to find it in the writing of some of those you know as good fellows. It is true that they are hail fellow well met on the surface but underneath they limit their close friends to a very small group.

If by any chance you feel that you do not see the distinction of this squared or triangular loop as clearly as you might, then study the writing of June Knight, the talented

movie performer. Here the *y* and *g* are made with long slender lower loops, not at all square. These long loops have a story all their own, which you will learn when you will come to it in a later chapter.

Unlike the loops in both the *g's* and *y's* made by Tom Keene, and June Knight, there is another interesting story revealed by Joe E. Brown in his well-rounded or triangular loops. His loops are large, revealing an active imagination. He thinks rapidly, forms conclusions instinctively and when he is interested, he will study and analyze a problem carefully. He has poise and emotional balance, the ability to "take it on the chin" without calling for help. He has one great goal in life. Justice. Joe is a builder of air castles about which he becomes enthusiastic, as he shows by the sweeping crossbars for his *t*'s. He is also persistent, tying his *t* in *what* with a knot. Keep one thing in mind when you see Joe E. Brown, the famous comedian.

He thinks and acts for himself, which is just as much a mark of leadership today as it has been in the past.

Students who have studied with me at various times during many years have frequently asked, "What is the difference between pen writing and pencil writing?" This is not an idle question, although it is answered easily enough. Pencil writing may look more careless, but the mind that guides the pen is the same one that guides the pencil, and all writing is a reflection of mental habits. This is the reason you can analyze and tell even the most intimate details about a writer's character. The mental habits show in the strokes, no matter whether those strokes are made with pen, pencil, chalk or some other writing instrument.

So far as that goes you do not need to write with your hands in order to provide an accurate pen sketch of yourself. In another chapter you will find four different specimens of writing, none of them *handwriting*, each telling the truth about the individual writer.

Living with real people, comparing what you know about them with what you learn from their handwriting, will increase your skill in digging the facts out of a specimen of writing. I have found this true, so that even today each new piece of handwriting is to me something interesting and stimulating. It represents the picture of a new personality, new acquaintance and friend who may prove to be a very unusual personality.

You may even discover someone with potential talent that is undeveloped, and by reading his handwriting you may be able to give him the encouragement he needs to go ahead and make a place for himself in the world. It was during his early days in Hollywood that Gary Cooper sent me his writing. The warm friendliness of his forward strokes convinced me that he would create a tremendous following of picture fans. Then too I found that he made

n's and *m's* like small *w's*. This is the sign of ability to think rapidly, to understand readily. The two traits of character were so clearly expressed that it was easy to see a great future for the young actor.

One thing in particular is prominent in Gary Cooper's writing. This is the marked forward slant of the writing which contains highly interesting revelations, that you will find explained in detail in a later chapter along with rules which you can use on your own writing, or the writing of another.

Or you may find a writer with *g's* made like the figure *8* as in this specimen where the word *give* starts with such a

character. When you find such a *g,* look for a talented person. It may be that the writer will lack education, but there will be an underlying interest in culture that will stand out in the face of lack of training and education. What is more, during my own lifetime I have seen writers with this figure *8* formation for the *g* rise from utter failure to success. They needed the encouragement of knowing that they might do something with their lives, and when given insight into the natural ability that shows in their handwriting they have had the courage to fight on and eventually lift themselves to a point of success.

I suggest that, in order to get the most accurate picture of a person through his handwriting, you make your analysis from many samples written by the same person at different times and under varying circumstances.

CHAPTER III

EMOTIONAL EXPRESSION AND DEPTH

STUDY the Emotional Chart carefully. This is your *Emotional Expression* or your *How You Feel* chart. Laid over a line of writing, it tells you how the writer of the specimen feels. Each of the slanting lines tells a different story

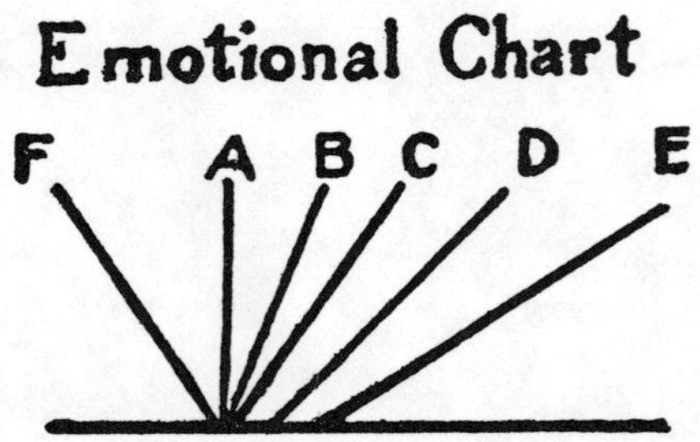

about a writer's expression of feeling. For this reason you should study this chart thoroughly and make one for your own use. In order to do this, take a piece of transparent paper or celluloid, and place it over the printed chart on this page. Draw the base line, which represents the base line of writing. Then draw with a firm hand the slanting lines as well as the upright line. Make an exact copy of the chart as it is printed on this page, using firm strokes, so that when you have completed the chart it will be exactly like the printed one.

When you have done this, you are ready to start analyzing handwriting. You may start on your own writing, or on a page of writing done by some friend, or even that of a stranger. You have specimens included in this chapter, bits of writing of men and women who have made names for themselves, and with whom you may be familiar. This gives you excellent practice material because they have been chosen to illustrate various points by the chart. On the other hand there is nothing better for study than your own writing, which may surprise you by its revelations of traits you have never recognized.

I make this recommendation because it is very true that there are few people who really understand themselves. They have a general idea of their make-up through the criticism or praise of their friends; they have heard time and again of faults which they may or may not have, but which some member of the family is certain exist. All of these things enter into the self-knowledge that the average person has and in a very great many cases this knowledge has to be corrected, because often what the individual knows about himself or herself is not the truth.

In order to determine the slant of your writing, lay your newly-made Emotional Expression chart over the writing to be studied, so that the base or unlettered line on your chart is also over the base line of your writing. If your paper is ruled, the base line of your chart will lie over the ruled line. If you are studying writing that is on unruled paper then place your Emotional Expression chart so that the base line of the chart will be under the line of writing.

Occasionally you may find a specimen where the first letter of the word starts on the base line and then slants upward, as in this specimen. In a case like this, turn the chart so that the base line will follow the upward slant of the word. In such a specimen the base line of the chart will lie directly under the word as indicated by the letter *B*.

Next, in order to determine the emotional expression of a writer, slide your Emotional Expression chart along the

line of writing until one of the lines of the chart, *B, C, D,* or *E* is directly over the first stroke of *m, n,* or the stem of the *d, t,* or *l* of the specimen you are studying. The slant revealed gives you the degree of emotional expression of the writer. In some cases you will find the writing registering between two of the lines of your Emotional Expression chart. In such a case you will know that the writer's emotional expression is between the two degrees of expression registered by the chart lines between which it appears.

Your first specimen revealing extreme emotional expression is shown in the writing of that star of the silent movies, the late William S. Hart. Mr. Hart succeeded in painting a clear picture of himself in only a few lines. He

was warmhearted, impulsive, quick to show exactly how he felt. You could get his immediate support by stirring his emotions. When his feelings were hurt, he showed it by the way he walked, by the look on his face, by the droop of his shoulders. He expressed how he felt and were you to put his writing under your Emotional Expression chart you would have an understanding of the greatness of the man, though you might never have seen him. Throughout his film career he was most at home when he was protecting the oppressed, helping those who were in danger, or responding to demands made upon his sympathy. Screen audiences sat tense as Bill Hart, astride his plains pony, came tearing over the desert or over the hills, to shoot it out with some desperado who was endangering the lives of innocent men and women. His friends say he was a great actor and the box office showed the tremendous pull he had on the heartstrings of millions of people. His writing reveals that he was living up to his natural inclinations when he was playing the emotional parts which made him famous.

If your own writing slants far to the right, toward the *E,* you will have sudden spells of *the blues* when everything looks dark and forboding. You may come down in the morning with the sun shining and the whole world filled with promise; suddenly you feel that the bottom has dropped out of things in general. Possibly you cannot put your finger on just why this is so, but if you turn to your Emotional Expression chart, you will get the answer. Your nature is a highly expressive one, you are swayed by your heart and not ruled by your head. Your sympathies are easily aroused, and many, many times you do things on the spur of the moment that you will regret later.

Your writing, with the *l's, d's,* and *h's* slanting up and far forward under the *E* line of your chart, puts you in the same emotionally expressive class as Bill Hart. Nature has given you the same ability to appeal to the emotions of people and to understand them. Furthermore, when you find other such specimens as you go along in your study of many different handwritings, you may be sure that those other writers share the same traits of character. Bill Hart became famous as an emotionally expressive actor. You, with the same emotional expression, have the ability to reach people just as he did. These other writers, with similar emotional expression, also have a valuable character trait if they develop their possibilities.

If you slant your writing far forward, you have a tendency to make many mistakes, for you do not use judgment. Your intentions may be the very best, but when it is a question of judgment or sympathy, your sympathy will rule. Keep this in mind, because when you find it in the writing of another person, you have the secret of how to appeal to that person. Touch his or her sympathy and you have gained a friend or a supporter.

Many of my clients and students during the past thirty years have called this a fault, but it is not. With a highly emotional nature, you have the ability to appeal to people, to arouse their sympathy or interest; you have a wealth of possibilities in this trait, provided you use it with care. Of course, because it is a valuable trait, it is also dangerous if misused. Years ago, when lecturing in New Orleans under the auspices of the Loyola University radio station WWL, Father Abell, of the University remarked to me that I rarely told people much about their faults. He said it gently and kindly, and knowing him as a man of sincere character, I gave his comment careful consideration. During the many years that I have been analyzing handwriting, I have found very few real faults, but I have found a great number of excellent character traits which have been seriously misused. This is true of great emotional expression. If you let it get the best of you, these emotional storms can sweep you into despair just as they can sweep you to the heights of success. You are ruled by your heart, by your sympathy, by your feeling, and if you let those feelings go without control or direction, they are just as dangerous as a streamlined train in motion without an engineer. Guided, controlled, they are mighty factors that can lead directly toward success.

Eugene V. Debs, one-time leader of the Socialist party in the United States, had this tremendous emotional ap-

peal. Use your Emotional Expression chart on his signature and you will find that the first stroke of the letter *b* in *Debs* slants far forward. The whole writing, for that matter, is extreme in its slant, and Eugene V. Debs was an extremist. His sympathies ruled him. He saw men and women living in poverty, going hungry, suffering, and he wanted to do something about it. So he went out and appealed to others, stirring them up, pleading the cause of those who had aroused his sympathy. When the World War came along, he fought war, he talked against it, he wrote against it, until finally his extreme emotionalism caused him to be sentenced to a federal prison. Throughout all of his experiences, though, the men opposed to him never questioned the sincerity of the man. They opposed his tremendous emotionalism, fought his ability to stir up the people; they insisted that he was a dangerous leader, but they did not doubt his honesty, or his sympathy.

When Debs wrote,

> "While there is a lower class, I am in it,
> While there is a criminal element, I am of it,
> While there is a soul in jail, I am not free."

he expressed the spirit of the man, and his handwriting tells the same thing. While there was someone hungry, suffering, discouraged, he was hungry, suffering, and discouraged, also. He felt what others felt; he pleaded for the underpaid, the overworked, the men and women who did not have a chance. He headed a political movement, but Eugene V. Debs was not a politician; he was an extremist in his sympathies, in his responsiveness to suffering of any kind. This is the history of the man, but without knowing anything about what he believed, or the way he lived, it would take only a few moments to determine the truth by putting your Emotional Expression chart over the Debs' signature. This single line tells the story and a great deal more besides. It tells of self-reliance, of tremendous energy, of tenacity of purpose, and of a strong bent for literary expression.

Other great political leaders and reformers and social workers have shown the same striking forward slant, and wherever you find it, you may expect the writer to exhibit his emotions and to respond immediately to emotional influences. If your own writing slants forward under slant *C, D,* or *E,* or between any two of these letters, your heart, not your head, will rule, and the greater the slant, the greater your response to emotional influences.

On the other hand, if you find that your writing does not slant, but is vertical or nearly vertical, between *A* and *B,* you do not let your heart rule your actions, and your display of feeling will be held in check by your judgment. You have cool self-possession that influences you in all of your actions and interests. You ask yourself *Will it pay?,* or *Will it work?,* before you take any important step.

As you gain skill in determining the slant of handwriting, you will be surprised at many of your findings; also, you will have people asking you to "tell fortunes" from their handwriting. However, grapho-analysis is not fortunetelling, but on the contrary, it is scientifically opposed to fortunetelling. A man's writing does not tell what will occur in his life, but it does show how he will act under various influences. By the time you have completed reading this book and testing the rules which are given and illustrated, you will be able to pick up a stranger's specimen of writing and draw a very clear word picture of how that writer will act. You will know if he is truthful or deceitful, if he is stubborn or easily influenced. All of this is based on a scientific foundation and not on guesswork.

This simple Emotional Expression chart is one of the important foundation stones on which you will build all of this knowledge, so you should become thoroughly familiar with it. The following rules are provided to impress upon your mind the facts you have already studied in this chapter.

1. In writing where the forward strokes of *t, d, h, l, k, m,* or *n* are under or between the letters *A* and *B* on your chart, the writer will be ruled by judgment, and will not show emotional reactions in an extravagant manner.

2. When you find the slant strokes between *B* and *C,* the writer will respond to emotional influences and show feelings readily, but will not be extreme in such reactions.

3. Writing that registers from *C* to *D* is evidence of a very expressive nature.

4. Writing that registers from *D* to *E* is evidence of an intensely expressive nature, close to hysteria when deeply stirred; given to marked periods of despondency which in turn give place to equally marked cheerfulness and delight.

5. Writing that registers from *A* to *F* is evidence of a reserved nature. It is the writing of one who prefers to stay in the background. Such a writer's judgment will be severe, especially if the writing is very light. Where the writing is very heavy the writer will carry grudges or the memory of hurt feelings and embarrassment for a long time, but will not make any show of the feeling.

So far you have learned about emotional expression or the show of feelings, and how to determine emotional expression. There is more to emotion, however, than mere expression. There is *depth* or *permanence*. Many of those who show the greatest emotional excesses have the least enduring of emotions. Their pleasures and disappointments are fleeting. During the period of the emotion the expression is intense, but like a thunderstorm that rolls up in a half hour and is gone in another thirty minutes, such emotions may not be lasting. You have found that both the writing of William S. Hart and Eugene V. Debs show great emotional expression. There is something more, however, to these signatures than the emotional expression. The lines of writing are very heavy. This shows emotional depth or permanence of feeling.

This is illustrated clearly in the chart. The second upright line in this chart is very heavy, and parallels a light

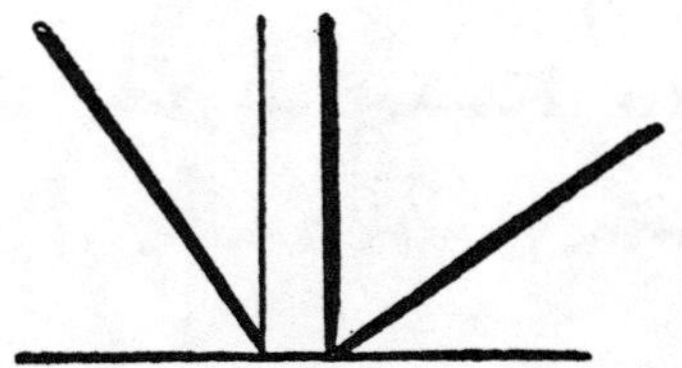

line. This light line shows poise, but there is no great depth of feeling in such a stroke. On the other hand the second upright stroke is heavy, and if this were writing it would indicate a lasting and constant emotional force. These two vertical strokes show the comparison between light, or short-lived, and deep, or long-lived, emotions. Heavy writing shows deep and lasting emotions. Light writing reveals short-lived emotions. These two rules are just as important as the five preceding ones, which have to do with emotional expression.

There is a difference between emotional expression and the duration of an emotion, and you will do well to familiarize yourself with the difference before going on to the next chapter.

In the following specimen the writing is straight up and down or vertical, lacking slant. You know, from the use of your Emotional Expression chart, that this writing shows poise and emotional balance. But in addition you

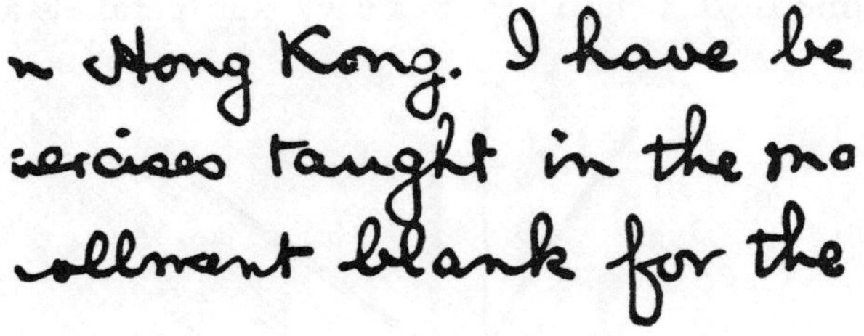

also have heavy pen strokes which show great depth or constancy of character. This means that the writer will be very deeply and lastingly hurt or pleased, but that he will not show it, because his emotional *expression* is not nearly so strong as his *ability to feel.*

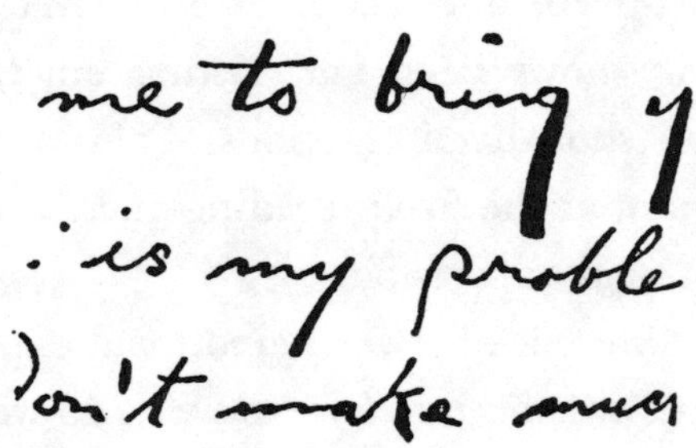

In the specimen above the writing is almost vertical, but the strokes, with the exception of the downstrokes, are very light, which means that the writer possesses poise and emotional balance, but in addition that his emotions are not lasting.

This variation of heavy and light strokes with writing that slants in varying degrees to the left or right presents endless possibilities for understanding people, and the emotional secrets which you will reveal in your experiences in handwriting analysis will be extremely interesting.

It was in Hollywood that I found one of the most interesting specimens of heavy, vertical writing, revealing judgment and deep emotions, ever submitted for analysis. The writer had made some success on the stage, and had been offered a part in Hollywood, but had refused to make terms. Nancy Smith, one of the most famous of Hollywood publicists, for whom I had made many analyses, sat behind her desk, and told the story. "I believe he has talent," she said. "I believe that you will find his writing interesting, and I would like to have you put down on paper just what you find. I need it, and I think he needs it, too."

That was the first time I saw Douglass Montgomery's writing. I took it to my hotel, studied it, and made my report, with rather more than a little satisfaction. Young Montgomery had talent, he had an underlying emotional force that had the strength to make him a great actor. He had judgment, shown clearly by his vertical strokes, while the heavy writing revealed his depth of feeling. His long downstrokes revealed his ability to go through difficulties until he reached success, while the breaks between the letters added their bit to the picture of his talent.

My report ran into several pages. I mailed it without meeting the young actor. Indeed, I have never met him, but his fans in both America and England may know now that his writing revealed his possibilities before he had ever taken a single part on the screen.

It is always that way. This next specimen is worth studying for the very same reason. Put your Emotional Expression chart over the writing and you will find that the *d*-stem, the *h* in *shall,* and his *t* all slant far forward to the point

that they reveal hysteria. This writer was a young dancer in Hollywood. He had real chances for success, but in a period of melancholy attempted to commit suicide. Not once, but twice. He was going through the slough of despondency that engulfs high-strung natures now and then, when they cannot see the brighter side of life. The writing, showing deep emotions as well as intense expression, reveals clearly the utter extremes to which the young fellow would go.

Keep this in mind when you meet people whose writing slants so far forward. They have all of the possibilities of great emotional appeal, but they sometimes pay for those gifts with intense suffering; they may experience the most bitter regrets that are without foundation; they frequently see everything black when it is not black, and very often may do things of a desperate nature.

In selecting writing for your study in this chapter I have

I hope this signature will help you and your work

Clara Bow

presented two other interesting specimens. One is the writing of Clara Bow, who submitted these two lines at a time when she was the great "It" girl of the country. Her name was in bright lights from the Pacific to the Atlantic, but these two lines show clearly her lack of interest in fame. Sometimes the strokes slant forward, but just as quickly they slant backward. Sometimes she was expressive, but almost at once she lost interest or changed to cool reserve. One minute she wanted to be a success, but the next she was tired of it all. Like a ship without a guiding hand she turned one way and then another, always looking for something, she knew not what. Clara Bow revealed in this writing that she wanted to be more than the "It" girl. She wanted love, wanted someone who could understand her, someone with whom she could be happy. If you were a Clara Bow fan, if you remember her flaming personality, you can take this writing and see for yourself what a home and family mean to her now. Screen writers wonder why she does not return to pictures. Her fans ask the same question. Two lines of writing, penned when she was a star, give the answer. She wanted love and she has found it.

Read Boris Karloff's writing for yourself and you will appreciate his talent as I did. You will see too that though his analysis was made when he was packed and ready to start for England, where he was to play in a new picture, he took time to send his greetings and to tell me that handwriting had revealed his personality amazingly. When you analyze his writing under your Emotional Expression

chart you will see that doing such a generous thing was merely being natural. He wanted to be friendly.

CHAPTER IV

YOUR SELF-RELIANCE AND DETERMINATION

WHEN Bernarr Macfadden, head of Macfadden Publications, Inc., publishers of many popular magazines, was new in that field he sent me his first letter. He had only

Sincerely,

Bernarr Macfadden

one publication, *Physical Culture Magazine,* that was at that time only a bit too large to fit into a man's coat pocket. He was almost entirely unknown, but when 1 examined his signature it was a simple matter to be absolutely certain of his success. Although handwriting does not foretell the future, it does indicate exactly the kind of material that a man has out of which to build his own future, and the young publisher, almost unknown at the time, had self-reliance, a vast reserve of it. This was indicated by the long, sweeping stroke under his signature.

You had the same kind of stroke under the signature of the late William S. Hart. It also appeared under the signature of Eugene V. Debs, and you will find it under the signature of many men and women who are successful. Furthermore, here is something you can depend upon: You will never find it under the signature of a weakling, a man who is constantly asking favors, or crying on your shoulder. A sweeping stroke under a signature is certain evidence of self-reliance. Such a writer will go to the bank instead of to his father-in-law to borrow money; he will shoulder blame if it is coming to him. He does not constantly apologize when no apology is needed.

This does not mean that he will have all the virtues in the dictionary. Not by a long shot. He may be a crook, a liar, a colossal scoundrel, but he stands on his own feet. He isn't crawling around on his belly begging for crumbs from someone's table. Not such a man. He may go down in defeat but he never stays down.

In the years since that first encounter, I have had many letters from Bernarr Macfadden, and he has invariably used the sweeping stroke that was such a prominent part of his signature many years ago.

It was also a characteristic of the Houdini signature, and no one living who ever saw the famous escape expert and

magician in one of his performances would question for a moment his self-reliance. Even as a boy Houdini met disappointments and misfortunes without flinching. The trait was strengthened, and this signature, written just before his death, revealed at once his strongest character-istic. Of course he had other prominent traits: a quick, spitfire temper, great tenacity of purpose, and a flair for the unusual. He loved the bright lights and the applause of his audience. It was meat and drink to him, but under-neath it all there was the self-reliance that he revealed every time he wrote a letter or signed his name.

Again, when E. Phillips Oppenheim sent me his writing from Paris, the first thing I noticed was the amazing self-reliance of the man. The stroke was not long, but it was there, revealing that just as long as the novelist was interested in a subject, he would be self-reliant in his views and actions.

handwriting rule is of little significance, for the simple reason that I do not write one letter a week by hand & my fingers are naturally stiff.

Sincerely I am
E. Phillips Oppenheim

Of course all self-reliant people are not men. There are women who have just as much of this quality of character as any man has ever had. Further, it is just as plain in a woman's signature as in a man's. Take the signature of Mary Stewart, successful candy manufacturer who sub-

mitted a handwritten letter for examination during her early days in business. As in the case of most famous or successful people, Mary Stewart's request for an analysis of her handwriting came without blare of trumpets or show of success, simply written on plain paper. Her signature showed sensitiveness as her greatest single handicap, fortunately offset by cool judgment. Her enthusiasm was expressed by the sweeping cross strokes for her *t's*, but it was her entirely self-reliant nature that gave me the greatest assurance of her success. The underbar was strong, showing that the writer could and would meet emergencies.

All of these and other facts went into the personal report which was mailed just the same as any other specimen. For a long time I kept copies of all reports, but the thought that those filing cabinets crowded with copies of what I had told men and women in confidence might fall into strange hands, caused me to burn all of the old copies of reports and never to make another copy except in cases of legal or medical analyses where the report was to be studied by several persons.

Following out this plan, the Mary Stewart analysis was completely forgotten, until I found a letter of thanks in my mail. Along with the letter Mary Stewart submitted printed evidence that she was capable of being a success. Newspaper stories had already covered her achievements as an executive, verifying what her handwriting had told so clearly.

Mary Stewart was a candy manufacturer, a business woman, but the same self-reliance, the same ability to meet life squarely without alibis or apologies is in the handwriting of Ruth St. Denis, world-famous dance artist and teacher.

It is, in fact, a characteristic that you may find in any class or group of people, because there is no restriction on self-reliance. Farmers and bankers and brokers have all had it, and when you find an under-the-signature bar such as you have in these signatures you can look for self-reliance in the writer. It was this trait, and the strong upward slant in his writing that first attracted my attention to the work that Albert G. Burns, founder of the Inventors Congress, was doing.

It has been a good many years since Burns, who was then a small business man in Pennsylvania, sent me his writing. He was skeptical, but he was also curious. He was willing to see how much there was to grapho-analysis, but until he found it was actually possible to analyze his hand-writing he did not intend to accept any hearsay. Naturally

I had never met the man and knew very little about him, but his handwriting showed both self-reliance and optimism. The latter trait was expressed by the way in which he wrote his signature uphill. Bernarr Macfadden had done the same thing years before. Both men believed in tomorrow and all of the future tomorrows. They were optimists, and as you go along, meeting men and women, you will always find that the writer who slants his signature uphill is a booster rather than a knocker. He believes in success and goes after it tooth and nail.

They may go down temporarily, but they climb back up, and keep climbing. Mr. Burns' history illustrates this clearly. He had a small business when I made his first analysis. He was making money, but not for long. He lost his business. Before that he had been a successful salesman, but he had given it up to go into business for himself. Things went badly after a time, but when they did, Burns lived up to his signature. He climbed out of the wreck and started over again. He simply would not stay down. Neither Macfadden nor Burns had money or influence when they started. Probably Macfadden did not dream of becoming one of the world's largest publishers, and it is just as certain that Burns did not plan to head an organization of inventors with thousands of members. Such plans would have seemed impossible, but both men had that which was more than rich or influential friends or a reserve of cash in the bank. They believed they could do something. They had the optimism to believe in doing their very best without asking other people for help. They were not interested in *pull,* but in *push.* They expected to make their own way in the world, and this quality, along with the optimism that shows so clearly in their handwriting, is undoubtedly the secret of their success.

Charles P. Steinmetz had the underscore under his signature. Boris Karloff and Warner Baxter both have it, and there are thousands of others in every walk of life who have this underscore in one form or another, positive evidence of self-reliance. You will find many handwritings that show this trait together with optimism. Sometimes you will find one but not the other, but when you find

them together you may be quite sure you have a specimen of writing of a very strong and very capable personality.

Sometimes you find another trait indicated by the signature underscore. This new trait is revealed in the flourish under the name of Lee Duncan, owner of the first famous motion-picture dog, Rin-Tin-Tin. Lee Duncan's

writing shows self-reliance, but it also reveals showmanship, a natural flair for recognizing what people want and
giving it to them.

In spite of the great self-consciousness, revealed by the
high final stroke in the capital *M*, the movie actor Monte
Blue revealed his self-reliance by this sweeping stroke

under his signature. He had to fight self-consciousness, but
he had the reliant spirit to do it. His self-consciousness
might be a handicap, but he would not be overcome by it.
In exactly the same way Bela Lugosi showed his own

ability to meet life fairly and squarely. His sweeping
stroke under the signature proved his self-reliance, and
added to it he showed determination by his downstroke
at the finish.

Both of these men mentioned above belonged to the

Hollywood movie colony, whereas K. V. Iyer is a teacher of physical training in British India. He is an optimist, and he is self-reliant. His writing slants upward and the understroke is strong, and doubles back upon itself. They are three widely different personalities, separated by race

and distance, but they all possess the underlying trait of confidence, of ability to face life squarely. No matter where a man lives or what he does, if he possesses self-reliance it will show in his writing.

You will find such people interesting to know, although not any more so, possibly, than those men and women whose writing shows *determination* as one of their strong points. Very determined persons are usually interesting, especially when you have studied their writing so that you understand them and their determination.

Determination is shown in downstrokes. Dolores Del Rio illustrates the point in the downstroke of her *g* but it is even stronger in the word *submit* in the line above, because in this case the *t* is brought down in an exaggerated formation, thereby supplying the long downstroke revealing her determination. In the small *a* following she repeats this same exaggeration, so that altogether even these few strokes show a character that is almost entirely controlled by her determination. These thick downstrokes,

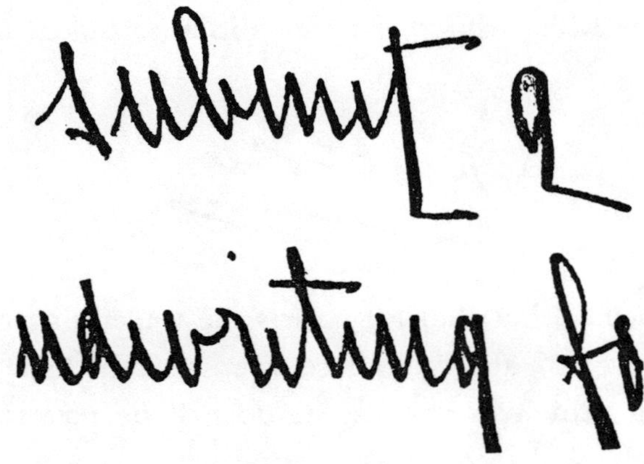

no matter where you find them, are evidence of the amount of determination which the writer possesses. Study handwriting specimens of your friends and so prove this rule or any other rule you find in this book.

Sometimes you will find determination revealing itself in the most unexpected places. I shall never forget my own experience with the handwriting of Oliver Hardy of the famous Hardy-Laurel team in Hollywood. I had not met Oliver Hardy and knew nothing about him beyond the screen stories until his note requesting an analysis was delivered to me. There was determination in that writing. Judgment, rapid thinking, keen sensitiveness, self-reliance, a flair for showmanship, all of these were there also, but greater than any one of them was the marked determination in the *y's* and *g's*. Count the determination strokes for yourself. They are in *my*, in *handwriting*, in *certainly* where the *y* itself fades out but the determination holds its

own. In *reading,* the *g* is looped but the downstroke is strong, and the same thing is true in *Yours* where the heaviest stroke of the word is the long downstroke in the *Y*. If Oliver Hardy won screen fame, and every one of his fans will affirm his fame, he did it because of determination. He had what it takes to carry out plans and purposes. His determination is worth studying and making your own if life has not given you all you want.

The principle of these downstrokes is logical. A determined person has a goal; such a person travels in a straight line. It is not necessarily a matter of going forward, but it is a matter of completing a given task or purpose. A straight downstroke is accordingly the natural way to express this mental trait, and as you examine the handwritings of your friends you will find that it is a rule you can rely upon at any time.

roaming

In the word *roaming* the downstroke of the g is exaggerated, although you may find writers who make their downstrokes just as long in proportion to their other

tenacity

writing. Such a long downstroke means determination that carries through no matter what hinders.

It is long-lived determination, whereas in *tenacity* and

in *your* the downstroke is short. Such writers are determined at the beginning of a venture, but if there are

hindrances, and things go hard with them, they drop out.
Such determination belongs to the type of man who is a
good beginner, but a very poor finisher.

On the other hand *today* illustrates not only determination by the downstroke, but also reveals another trait of
character in the tight little loop at the finish. When you

find a *y,* or *g* ending in such a narrow loop you can be
sure that the writer is extremely exclusive in regard to
friends. A boy who makes such loops rarely has more than
one chum, and as he grows older may be a good mixer in
an impersonal way, but will still have few trusted or intimate friends.

The unsigned specimen on page 42, which begins
me to bring reveals determination out of all proportion to
the other traits of character possessed by the writer. This
determination is so great that it "shows off" and so becomes the center of the writer's personality. When he at-

tempts anything he does it with so much determination that the trait of character takes the center of the stage. You will not find many such writers, but if or when you do, there is only one decision you can reach. Their determination is the outstanding quality of their natures.

Four other unsigned specimens are included here, each illustrating in a distinctive way the strong downstrokes

revealing determination. In the specimen above there is an exceptionally heavy downstroke in the word *you*, and another in *guilty*. The *y* in *you* makes a small loop, rather than a large one, indicating that the writer clings to ideas and purposes. Tenacity to ideals and to ideas shows up in hitherto unsuspected persons, that is, unsuspected by anyone who has not analyzed such a writer's handwriting. When you have analyzed the writing and found this characteristic you will know what to expect.

In this specimen you have more downstrokes indicating determination, and if you look closely you will find

the least little *tick* or *hook* at the finish of both *y's* and
also the *g*. This writer is not as tenacious as the writer
in the preceding specimen, but the trait is there and will
grow if encouraged.

In this handwriting the hook in *y* in *Maybe* is made
forward, and does *not* indicate that the writer has tenacity.

It has a meaning all its own, and a very important one which you will discover in a later chapter. Remember that a tenacity hook at the end of the downstroke in *y* or *g* must be turned to the left, and not to the right.

The writing in the specimen above is unusually interesting because it reveals so very many outstanding characteristics. It shows persistence, deceit, an inferiority complex that battles the equally strong determination, care about details, creative ability, and artistic talent. If you study the *y*, you find that it is another illustration of a narrow loop indicating clannishness or great care in selecting close friends and associates. The downstroke of the *y*, however, is a determined downstroke, just as much as it would be if the loop were lacking.

It is these little hooks and tick strokes that provide the details in a character, while such strong lines as the downstrokes revealing determination provide the skeleton of the most important characteristics. For this reason it is important that you give attention not only to prominent signs, but to the smaller and less noticeable ones as well if you are really to understand and use grapho-analysis in getting a clear picture of a writer.

For instance, in this single chapter you have learned how to determine *optimism, self-reliance,* varying degrees of *determination,* and also how to recognize *tenacity of purpose.* These are all important traits and you will find them very often as you study handwritings. When you do find them you may easily have a key to a personal problem. Remember as you make these studies that it is very rarely that one single trait of character rules all others, but that the various strokes expressing individual characteristics found in a single handwriting are each affected in some degree by others. A very determined writer will, for instance, seem even more determined if he is also tenacious. He will be determined, but his tenacity will cause him to cling even more earnestly to his purpose. Also, when you find that a writer is both determined and enthusiastic, it will seem that each trait is stronger because the enthusiasm supports the determination, and at the same time the determination adds to the enthusiasm.

You will find that it is such variations, additions, and subtractions that make the study of handwriting so fascinating. The more you analyze strange writings, the more you will learn the law of evaluation so that your findings gain in accuracy as you practice your rules of analysis.

There is great determination in the long downstroke of the *R* in the Irene Rich signature.

It is also in the writing of Ramon Novarro, shown above, about whom you will find an interesting story later. It is in the *y* of *By*, of Santie Sabalala's specimen.

Santie Sabalala was, incidentally, one of the most unusual of many unusual clients. The specimen of writing which he very graciously asked me to keep as a souvenir consisted of the verses which are included here.

The Cannibal Feast

By

Santha Bahalala

THE CANNIBAL FEAST
A fierce little man,
    all muddy and brown,
Rattling a rattle
    with a terrible frown
Glared at the captives
    down at his feet
Fat, plump, juicy meat.
    Rattle, Rattle, Rattle.

"Down to the pool
    and do not drown
These prizes sleek
    in my home town,"
Said the fierce little man
    with a smile bitter sweet,
As he filed his teeth
    and pounded his feet.
    Rattle, Rattle, Rattle.

They may not strike you as outstanding poetry, but they are a real accomplishment. According to his own story, Santie Sabalala was born a cannibal, the son of savages who still practiced the weirdest of weird rites, deep in the jungle. Captured by white explorers, he was taken to England and educated, not only in the grade schools, but was given a college education by his benefactor. Then he set out upon his own, determined to become a journalist in the white man's world. It was at that time he submitted his writing for an estimate of his literary talent. I told him the truth, just as I found it, and also pointed out that his handwriting already revealed the physical decay that was shortly to end his life. Santie Sabalala had the determination, he had the will to do, but the change from the jungle to the white man's world was too great. It was utterly impossible to look at this writing and see a long period of success ahead. It simply was not in the writing, but Sabalala faced the revelations of his handwriting like a soldier. "I am staggered to the bottom of my soul," he said, "at your keen and accurate reading. It really was like witchcraft. I have to tell you that you are the first person in civilization who has been able to get behind my African mind."

Sabalala wrote until the finish, even when he knew the end was coming. He had to go ahead. Examine his writing and you will understand why he could not quit.

CHAPTER V

SOME IMPORTANT CONSONANTS AND THREE VOWELS

You will find that small letters are important and inter-esting because they tell you intimate details. Take these six *d's* for instance. The first one shows sensitiveness, but

in spite of the sensitiveness the writer is independent. The loop reveals the *sensitiveness,* and the short stem indicates the writer's *independence.*

The second *d* shows *resentment to imposition,* rather a weak resentment, and more pride with the same sensitive-ness. The two letters look very much alike, but they are not. The first is short-stemmed and the second is taller, which indicates more pride and also a greater inclination to follow established customs rather than to create new plans and courses through life. A still taller *d*-stem would indicate more pride and an even greater inclination to do what the crowd does rather than to act independently.

The height of the stem is the main difference between the two, but there is another difference that is important. There is a straight stroke starting at the line before the circle part of the second *d*. This straight stroke, starting at the line, has a value all its own. It shows a readiness to feel imposed upon, and to resent that imposition. Such a writer is always ready to feel that others are planning to take some advantage, and prepared ahead of time to resent any such move. Such writers are always carrying a chip on their shoulder either as a result of an exaggerated idea of their own importance, or from some other cause. Sometimes children who have grown up in poverty or cruelty develop this resentment as they grow older. Others, pampered and cared for as children, develop this trait when they are compelled to face the stark realities of life. There may be any one of many causes for the resentment of imposition, but the point that counts here is that when you find a writer beginning words with an inflexible stroke starting at the base line of the writing, you can expect to find a character that is on the defensive most, if not all of the time. If the first stroke is weak, as in this case, the resentment will be weak, and if the stroke is thick and heavy, the resentment will be strong.

The flourished *d* is a flirtatious one, while the very tall-stemmed letter in the second row shows vanity. Whenever you find a *d*-stem that is out of proportion to the circle part of the letter, that writer is certain to prove vain.

This is true even when the stem is made in two lines as in the fifth *d*. It may be a loop rather than a straight stem. The loop or double lines are not what count so far as determination of vanity is concerned. It is the extremely high *d*-stem that reveals the vanity, just as the double lines in the fifth *d* are a sign that the writer takes his own good time. Try to rush him and see how effective your efforts are. You will find that you have wasted your energy for the very simple reason that any writer who makes either the *t* or *d* with a double stem is deliberate, sluggish, lazy. He may start a task without delay, but he will drag it out indefinitely. He does not procrastinate, but he does not see the reason for hurrying. He moves slowly.

The wigwam shape of the last *d* is a sign of stubbornness. You will find the same rule in Chapter VI, where you analyze the letter *t*. The wigwam, or inverted *v*, always shows stubbornness. No matter what other fine traits the writer possesses, there are times when he will not yield a point, even when his own better judgment tells him to do so. You will find such *d's* in the writing of men and women who claim credit for being *firm,* but who are nothing more nor less than stubborn. Such writers may be generous, kindly, loyal, truthful, but all of these traits do not wipe out stubbornness if that quality is shown in the writing. You may wait a long time to see it expressed but it is there and will come to the surface eventually.

The specimen above is the writing of a young man who was attached to my staff for years. Reserved, deeply and expressively emotional, he was also exceedingly vain about many things. This vanity shows in the *d* in the word *and* as he has written it, while his independence of thought and action is revealed by the *d* in *forward*. Many times you will find two different formations of one letter in a single line or page of writing, but this does not mean that either one is a mistake. Each tells its own story, and you must take the two revelations and put them together if you are going to get the whole truth. These two *d's,* for example, show that this young man was vain, but that he also thought for himself, acting independently rather than always doing the accepted thing.

Another short-stemmed *d* revealing independence is used by Reginald Denny in his signature. His wide-open

d shows frankness, ease of verbal expression, while the short stem of the letter registers his ability to think for himself, make his own decisions. You will find both of these specimens interesting, both worth repeated examination.

In the Dan Beard signature you will find the same independent *d's*. This is the specimen the famous leader of the Scouts sent me for examination. It was an interesting report to make because it showed so clearly the ability of the man to think and act for himself. His *d*-stems, short to the point of stubbiness, showed his independence, and his *m's* and *n's* revealed his desire to learn, to get facts, and then to analyze what he had learned. The combination of these traits with cool judgment gave him qualities of leadership. He could get facts without bias. He would weigh such facts, and reach his own conclusions, after which he could independently follow them out.

If, by any chance, you find that you make short *d*-stems, you can be satisfied that you act and think independently of others, and that if you possess the ability to learn, to analyze what you learn, and to be fair, you have qualities of leadership. It will not be the same kind of leadership which created a following for Eugene V. Debs, whose writing you found in an earlier chapter. He was a great emotional leader, while Dan Beard shows judgment as the foundation for his success. This is an interesting difference and a very valuable one as well. All of our leaders cannot be emotionalists if our progress as a country is to continue. Each needs the other, and it is a wise character that recognizes this fact. A man who arouses emotional enthusiasm has his place, but he needs the man of judgment and analytical ability to help him, if his words and works are to endure.

Two other specimens of writing, each with a short *d*-

stem, are included here for your study and comparison. One is the signature of Claude Allister, motion-picture actor of silent film days.

The second is the handwriting of one of our most prolific women novelists who on at least two different occasions sent me her writing for analysis. She is highly sensitive, as you will find, while her large *g* loops show vivid imagination.

The specimen above has a retraced *d*-stem, and is well-proportioned as to height. The lady who wrote this began her career performing menial tasks in a small hospital. She did each task the best she could. As the years went by she worked, but she also studied, until when this was written, she was superintendent of a great hospital. This single letter *d* gives some of the explanation. She was proud enough to strive to succeed. She was still independent enough to think and act for herself. She succeeded where she might have sat down and cried, "I do not have a chance," and these four words tell why. Aside from the *d* there are other important revelations. The *o* is open, showing frankness. But there is another *o* that is almost closed, indicating that she was not only frank on occasion but just as capable of keeping to herself things that should not be told. She was emotionally expressive, and generous without extravagance. The way she wrote the *n* with the two points or inverted *v's* showed me her desire to learn, which I included in my analysis, along with other traits which you can find for yourself if you apply rules which you have already had, and others you will have in later chapters.

The following handwriting has very tall *d*-stems at the beginning of the word *decided,* and also in the word *find,* while the last two *d*-stems in *decided* are much shorter. This give you an interesting problem to analyze. Two high *d*-stems, and two shorter ones. When you have such an average you may be sure that the writer has high ideals,

e book.

Seller	List Price	Order Date
ng Tells You Your Friends and	$13.50	Jul, 6 2026

Shipping Instructions for MARKETSQ

Print this Packing Slip and enclose inside the front cover

Please ship this item no later than Thu Jul 16, 2026.

Ship to:

ALIBRIS APEX DC 76524048-57
APEX
800 AVONDALE AVE.
GRANDVIEW HEIGHTS, OH 43212-3473
UNITED STATES

PN #	Item ID	Alibris ID	Media Type	Title / Au
76524048-57	h04-1-27	B083662705	BOOK	What Han About Yo Famous P M.N. Bun

a high standard of integrity, but that he or she will act independently just the same. In such a case the personal

integrity is indicated by the high *d*-stems, provided of course that they are not abnormally high, and the independence of action and thought, by the shorter ones. If there are more short ones than tall ones, then you have evidence that the writer is going to act independently regardless of personal pride and integrity, when the circumstances are such that there is a conflict between the two traits.

In the next specimen you have some interesting *d's,* and a number of other letters which you will find particularly interesting after you have become familiar with the rules. You find the *i's* in the fifth line both dotted with round dots, indicating loyalty. Both *g* and *y* have well-rounded loops showing imagination, and the large-looped *p's* show a keen desire on the part of the writer for physical movement. Such a writer may be an active swimmer or participant in almost any kind of active sport requiring the vigorous use of the body muscles.

The next group of letters, in the specimen above, has three *b's* and three *c's,* each illustrating a special rule. In the first *c* as in *d,* an inflexible stroke at the beginning of the letter shows resentment to imposition. Very often such writers dot the *i* with short jabs of the pen, much like the last two in the specimen which follows below.

This is a natural combination. A writer who expects others to be unfair, one who is always alert through fear that someone will take advantage of him gets the habit of feeling that trouble is near. He gets ready for it, but in establishing this habit he sets up a condition of irritation that shows in the dotting of the *i* with the jab strokes. These traits of character are companions, and such a writer is more likely than not to show both of them.

The second *c* is tied at the heart, showing persistence. The third and final *c* is more interesting, because it gives you an entirely new trait of character, expressed by the hook at the beginning of the letter.

You will be surprised how many very agreeable persons have this beginning hook, not only before the *c* but before other letters at the beginning of words. Watch for it, and as you do, keep in mind that when a fisherman goes fishing he uses a hook to catch fish. He wishes to capture the fish, to gain possession of it, and so uses a hook. In exactly the same way a writer who makes many hooks at the beginning of words is reaching out to own, to possess. This hook does not mean stinginess, it does not indicate meanness or narrowness, but it does show that the writer is *acquisitive*. There are thousands of such writers who like to acquire, and who are just as ready to share with others, so you must not read into this rule something that is not true. A hook at the very beginning of a word, repeated often in a page of writing, is a certain sign of reaching out for ownership. Do not, however, confuse the initial hook at the beginning of a word with the hook at the end of a stroke or word. You will learn the significance of the final hook later.

As dependable an indicator as the initial hook is the sharp tick at the beginning of the *b* in the upper line. Check your own writing here. Do you have *tick* strokes before your *b* or *f* or before any other letter? If you do have such a stroke it is a sure sign that you have a temper. It is not excitability, or irritability, but plain old-fashioned temper. A *b* started with a circle loop shows jealousy. You may find this circle before the small *f, k, m, n, u, v,* or *w*. You may not find it often, or possibly not at all, for it has not appeared nearly so often as you might think in my many years of analyzing handwriting. Such writers may be generous, kindly, and friendly, or selfish and cold-blooded, but no matter what other traits they have, the small circle at the beginning indicates jealousy.

The third *b* has a very long beginning stroke, and a very high stem. Such a formation indicates idealism, and holds good whether you find it in *b*, or *f, h* or *l*.

You have already referred to the group of *i's*, but there

are additional rules governing this letter, illustrated in this specimen.

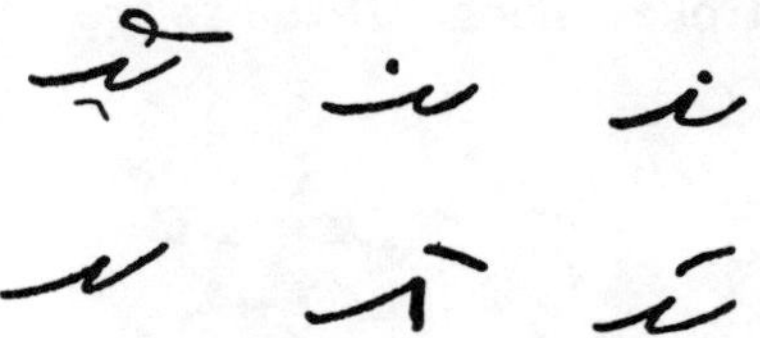

An *i* dotted with a circle and a dash shows irritability, and also individuality.

When the *i* is dotted back of the *i*-point, it is evidence of procrastination.

An *i* dotted with a circle or with a genuine dot, close to the point of the letter, indicates attention to details.

When the *i* dot is missing, there is no doubt that the writer does not care for, nor give attention to details. Even important matters are unimportant to such people, and for this reason writers who fail consistently to dot their *i's*, do not make good detail workers. They are not good private secretaries, accountants, record clerks, fine mechanics, or scientists. However, if such writers determine to do so, and have sufficient determination to carry out the purpose, they can develop this trait. This fact incidentally answers a question that my clients and students have asked many times. "If a person's personality changes, will his writing change?" There is only one answer. Writing is the reflection of mental habits, and as those habits change the personality changes, and as the change occurs the handwriting strokes change. If the *i's* are dotted like those

in this specimen, you can be absolutely sure that the writer is irritable and easily annoyed. Incidentally, this is a new rule and important, because these *i's*, dotted as they are, all show this trait. Also, no matter whether the writer is rich or poor, famous or not, the rule holds good.

In exactly the same way a circle dot, as in this specimen,

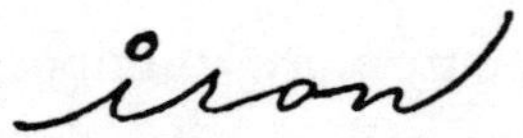

repeated many times in a page shows that the writer likes to be different, do things differently, and frequently cultivates unusual mannerisms. A woman who makes such circle dots will choose her clothing, house furnishings, even trinkets, with a desire to be different from her associates. If other women are wearing green hats, she will buy green, but will have a red feather or an unusual buckle because she must be different. The more circles you find in a page, the greater this individuality. It is not confined to women. Men make the circle dot, and it reveals the same thing in a man's handwriting, because after all there is no sex in writing.

mining

times

In the words *mining* and *times* the dots are placed very close to the *i* in each case. When you find the dot close to the point of the letter you have certain evidence that the writer gives attention to small details.

The word *iron* and each of the two specimens below provide variations you may expect to find in the size and location of the circle. For instance, if the circle is placed close to the point of the *i*, you must give it the same value you would if it were a dot placed in the same position.

This specimen, with the loops running into the line below and the line above, indicates a person who is interested in many things but is likely to scatter energy by jumping from one interest to another. The circle, however, has its own value, just as in the backhand writing which follows.

Here the lines are well separated, which indicates great determination, in addition to the characteristics shown by

the large circle for the *i*-dot. In this specimen the two *d's* are made with a backward twist or flourish indicating literary tendencies. These are merely an indication of such leanings, and not positive evidence of literary talent. Actual signs of literary ability are covered in another chapter. The main thing now is to clear up the character of the writer of the last specimen so that you will understand the writer's disposition. There is great determination in this writing, indicating that the writer will carry out a given purpose in the face of great obstacles. The individualism is shown by the circle dots for the *i*. A keen mind or rapid thinking is shown by the points of the *m* or *n,* as you already know. This writer's *m* qualifies, so you know he thinks rapidly. Summed up, this bit of writing shows a man who is determined, thinks rapidly, forms conclusions readily, has some literary inclinations, and possesses quite a share of individualism. His emotional nature you can work out for yourself.

It is in this way that you build up a complete picture of an individual, using each stroke for what it tells you, and fitting each bit or character trait into place until you have completed the picture.

In the word *handwriting* in the specimen above you have one dot far above the *i,* the other far forward and low, but they are both round dots. They are not arrows, or dashes, or blots of ink, but round, which is a sign of loyalty to ideals. If these dots were close to the point of the letter, they would mean loyalty and attention to details. If they were both written back of the point, they would indicate procrastination, the habit of putting off until later the thing that should or might be done at once.

You will find these round dots in unexpected places, because a man does not need to be rated as unusually good to have loyalty woven into his character. A man may be loyal to his ideas, and still make many mistakes. He may be loyal to his friends, and still choose those friends unwisely. He may possess outstanding faults, and still be very loyal. Your dictionary says that loyalty means faithfulness and very many people are faithful who are lacking in most of the characteristics usually credited to greatness.

You have already learned about emotional reactions, and emotions without expression. You have had many rules, and if you have memorized them at all you have already stored up sufficient knowledge of grapho-analysis to prove of very real help in studying your friends from their handwriting. In fact you may have discovered some unexpected things about yourself, thereby laying the foundation for a greatly improved personality. This will be entirely possible for many of those who read these pages. A handwriting analysis has many times revolutionized a writer's thoughts and habits; that is, the knowledge of personal habits has been so complete and so thorough that the subject of the analysis has, as it were, lifted himself by his own bootstraps, conquered serious character weaknesses, and strengthened other traits that needed encouragement. The case of one particular doctor stands out in my mind as a splendid example of what getting acquainted with one's self means. This doctor was very anxious to be grapho-analyzed. Then he wanted to study grapho-analysis. He knew he could master the principles, and his writing showed that he could, but that he would not study unless forced to do so. With this understanding he began work, but from the first he was an indifferent student. He was impulsive, possessed a very keen brain capable of learning, but was eager to rush on from one lesson to another without doing anything thoroughly. Finally, I deliberately made him so angry that he studied, simply to show me that he could master the lessons as I gave them to him. He lost sight of his original interest. He studied to convince me that he was right and that I was wrong. He mastered these rules that I have given you, but he did something more. He became acquainted with himself, and here is his experience in his own words:

"Grapho-analysis has really been a revelation. I thought I knew myself, but after the criticism on my part, I decided that I would apply grapho-analysis to my own handwriting. I did this with astonishing results. I thought I knew myself—but an analysis of my writing revealed to me many things that were not complimentary. I began to see myself in a new light. I found many traits that in the past I did not understand. I did something about all of this. I began to cultivate the opposite of the negative traits. I have not been entirely successful, but constant application has made it possible for me to curb my temper, sarcasm, emotional outbursts, and resentment. I feel much better for it all and am sure that I owe this new self-knowledge to the study of this science."

The doctor is only one of many who, by mastering the rules in this book, have gained a new understanding of themselves. Out of this knowledge they have created new and better personalities, merely by weeding out the handicaps discovered from the handwriting. You may have weaknesses of your own. Your friends may mention them, but you think they are nagging. However, if you discover them for yourself, through the use of these rules which you have already tested and found truthful, you will know yourself. If you find faults it is then a matter for you to

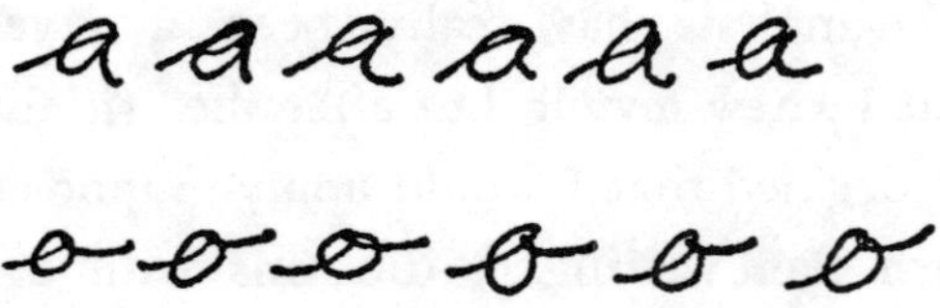

decide. You can keep them or get rid of them, conquer or cultivate them.

You have already learned that when an inflexible stroke

is used in starting a word, the writer "carries a chip on his shoulder." Therefore, when you examine this group of *a's,* you will recognize the trait revealed in the first two letters. This stroke shows a readiness to look after one's own interests far in excess of necessity; an alertness against trespassers when trespassing is not likely to occur. Further, if such a writer has a vigorous imagination, he will be likely to imagine additional reasons to be resentful and so live in a constant state of unrest. The remaining *a's* in the group do not start with straight, but curved strokes, and these do not indicate resentment. They merely help to form the circle at the top of the *a,* which shows self-deception. Such writers may not intend to lie, but they have the habit of not facing actual facts, or of overlooking important facts. Where the *a's* are repeatedly made with this initial circle, you may be sure that the writer misleads himself. The same rule applies to the *o,* and is true regardless of whether the letters are open or closed. Furthermore, when either the *a* or *o* is made with a circle at the beginning of the letter, and is also closed with a circle as in the line devoted to the *o,* the writer is actually deceitful. The slant of the writing does not affect the results, so that you have people who are deceitful on impulse and others cold-bloodedly so, intending to mislead.

While you are testing various *a's* and *o's,* you may find it interesting to keep an eye open for those with broken bases such as you find in the next specimen. Let us hope you do not find them, for if you do there is only one thing

to say: "Watch your step." More important, watch the writer and do not trust him. Avoid building up a friendship because these broken letters are a positive warning of danger that you cannot possibly afford to ignore. The writer lacks the definite moral sense that recognizes right and wrong. Such a writer will lie, betray friends and confidences, not because of impulse, but due to a lack of ability to recognize right from wrong. There are men and women filling important places in society who make these broken *a's* and *o's*, but no matter where you find them they are still dangerous. Avoid such persons. To trust them is to invite serious trouble, and this is true no matter how sweet-tempered, kindly, or docile they seem. In order to clear up one point that my students have frequently asked, these broken letters are not an indication of insanity as that term is usually used.

Changing now to a much pleasanter subject, you have the signature of Dr. M. J. Shields, a captain in World

War I, later raised to the rank of a Lieutenant Colonel, and one of the finest examples possible of a rapid, practical, and independent thinker. The last half of the letter *h* comes to a sharp point, the *i* is nothing but a point, while the small *e* is a closed point. Three sharp points in a row, and each reveals a desire to learn, to gather ideas, and the ability to comprehend immediately. The *d* is open, and the stem is short, which shows that the writer was able to think for himself.

My association with Dr. Shields was not as a grapho-analyst with a client, but man to man, as we served during the war. His handwriting says his judgment would be cool, and it was. He was generous, eager to have his men well cared for, but there was nothing of the reckless or impulsive in his makeup. What he did was done with a cool, calculating knowledge of the effort involved and the accomplishments to be gained. It is with deep respect that I honor him as one of the greatest men I have ever known, one of the finest examples of the ability to temper judgment with generosity, and as you study this signature you will find other traits, too, that added to his prestige among men.

You too may have friends who will rise in your esteem if you take the time to get the truth from their handwriting. Some of them may be truly great characters, even though they do not parade their virtues.

CHAPTER VI

SIXTEEN T'S TELL THEIR STORY

"Mind your p's and q's" may be a good enough rule ordinarily, but if you are going to get much out of handwriting, you should consider the letter *t* among the first, since it is the one letter in the alphabet that gives you the greatest number of indications of a writer's true character.

You will find the *t* crossed with long and short bars, with light and heavy ones. Sometimes the cross will be high on the stem, sometimes it will be crowded down until it is even with the tops of the small letters. Some writers cross the *t*-stem, others have the bar following the stem, still others write it before or in front of the stem, while some omit it altogether. In other cases you will find *t's* that are tied with a knot. There are countless variations,

each telling its own particular story, each revealing something important about the writer.

Sometimes too, you will find two or three different *t's*

in a single page, each revealing a trait of character, filling in important details of the word picture you get from the various strokes. In *tot,* for example, you have a *t* that turns back and ties with a knot. The same characteristic shows in the single *t* standing alone, and also in the word *mat.* It is true the knots are different, but they are knots, and a knotted *t* represents *persistence.*

The same sign shows in the signature of B. F. Mukati, famous Zoroastrian athlete and physical director from

India. I have never seen Mr. Mukati, but I know him. I know that he never admits defeat, and he is very self-reliant. The tied *t* shows his persistence, the underscore for his signature revealing the strong self-reliance. He finishes what he undertakes if it is humanly possible. He defies failure by never knowing or admitting failure. He goes ahead in spite of disappointments. All of this shows in his signature, and with it there is evidence of a good memory in the careful dotting of the *i,* just at the point of the stem or apex of the letter.

In much the same way that Mukati ties his *t,* the popular writer of western stories, Eugene Cunningham, ties his.

Study his writing, and you have not only a splendid collection of such *t's* but also *g's* and *d's* that show writing talent and inclination. It was when he had not more than a half dozen books to his credit that Mr. Cunningham sent me his writing. I wrote him that it certainly showed

Dear Bunker — You as I was wrestling for Houghton Mifflin very hell of a cold. I therefore. I very much Book ideas of yours; be asked to show my

his literary inclinations, but that even more important was his spirit of never saying "quits." Since then Eugene Cunningham has become a steady contributor to many magazines, with short stories appearing under as many as three names in a single issue of a magazine. He had talent, but more than talent he had persistence to overcome difficulties. Even if editorial refusals had come thick and fast, he would have fought on, because he has as much persistence as talent.

You will do well to study this Cunningham page because it tells so many interesting things about the man who tramped over Central America in order to gather the material for a book. It is far more than a study of *t's* and *g's* and *d's*, worth coming back to as you go along to new rules.

Another *t* that you will frequently find in examining the writing of others, and possibly your own, is the looped *t* as it occurs in *handwriting* and *returned*. In both places

the *t* is made as a loop and not as a stem. Such a *t* reveals certain sensitiveness. It may be a large loop or a small one, but the larger the loop the greater the sensitiveness. There are no exceptions to this rule. The writing may be in any language, in a crude or in a cultured handwriting, written with pen, pencil, or chalk, but wherever you find the looped *t* you have a sensitive writer. Such a person will feel slights that are not intended, will be hurt when there is no reason for such a feeling. It is a trait that creates much unnecessary unhappiness for those who have it, and my habit has been to call it to the attention of clients with the advice that they take themselves less seriously, that they forget the idea that people are intending to hurt them, and that they try to do for others instead of expecting too much from others.

When you find writing where the *t* is crossed above the stem you may be sure that the writer builds many air castles, dreams many dreams, and may have a far-distant goal to achieve. If the crossbars are thick and heavy as in the case of Charlotte Arthur, the goal is definite, clearly

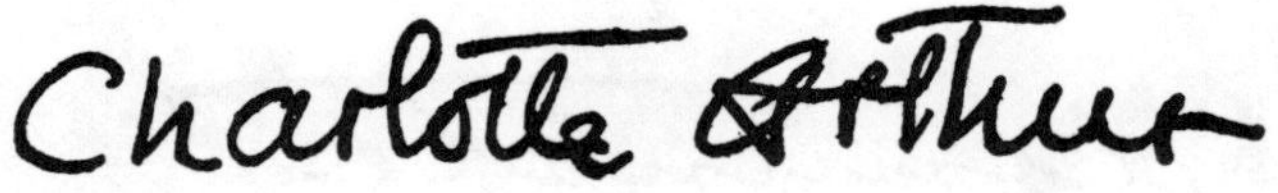

outlined, and the writer knows in which direction she is headed. It was a very great publishing house that sent me Mrs. Arthur's writing for a report, which they then sent on to her in England. As I had nothing but her signature on which to make my determinations, it was a pleasure to have her write to her publisher that "his report is extremely interesting. I can find no quarrel with any of his divinations. It is of course incomplete, but considering he had my signature alone to judge from, it is remarkable."

If, on the other hand, the *t*-bar is above the stem of the letter and is very light and short, you may know at once that the writer dreams, but does little more. The air castles are there, the hope of winning success sometime is there, but nothing more. There is no will to make the dreams

come true, no enthusiasm, as in the case of Arthur Stringer, to sweep these dreams into realities.

Arthur Stringer is enthusiastic about his purposes. He believes in them. He puts something back of them, and this shows in his handwriting.

Wherever you find long sweeping crossbars, you have enthusiasm. It shows in the long crossbar in the word *dominate*.

It shows again in the sweeping stroke used by Lowell Thomas in completing his capital *T* and by Ruth Chatterton, famous star of stage and screen, in crossing the three *t*'s in her signature.

In each case the crossbar is long, sweeping, indicating by its very length its value in your analysis. There are, of course, cases where you will find such crossbars exaggerated, as in the next four-line specimen. Here the long

crossbars are entirely out of proportion to all other strokes in the writing. This reveals not only enthusiasm, but more of an ostentatious streak, a desire to show off enthusiasm that does not actually exist. In a more evenly balanced style of writing these thick strokes would be evidence of genuine will power, but here the will power is a matter of pretense rather than actuality. As long as this writer is in a position where people are watching him, he will seem to exert a great deal of will power, but once by himself, his will power fades like dew before an August sun.

When you find the *t*-bar made like an arrowhead, as in this specimen, tread lightly. Such a writer has a razor-

edged tongue, and if he slants the arrowhead downward he wants what he wants when he wants it. He expects others to jump when he speaks. He does more than dominate. He domineers. There is no more dangerous sign in all of the *t*-bars than this, unless it is the one showing temper.

When you find a *t*-bar like the one in the handwriting, *situation if not,* the writer has a temper, a biting, explosive thing, that is without regard for others. If the bar is thick as the one after *not,* it is a lasting temper, instead of being nothing more than a terrific explosion. In any case, either the down-slanted arrow or the strokes revealing temper are unhappy traits, for such a writer must be handled with gloves. These writers do not care what they say, the more bitter and biting, the more they are pleased, until the outburst of temper is over. The next two specimens show the same danger signs.

This specimen has an added unfavorable sign. In this

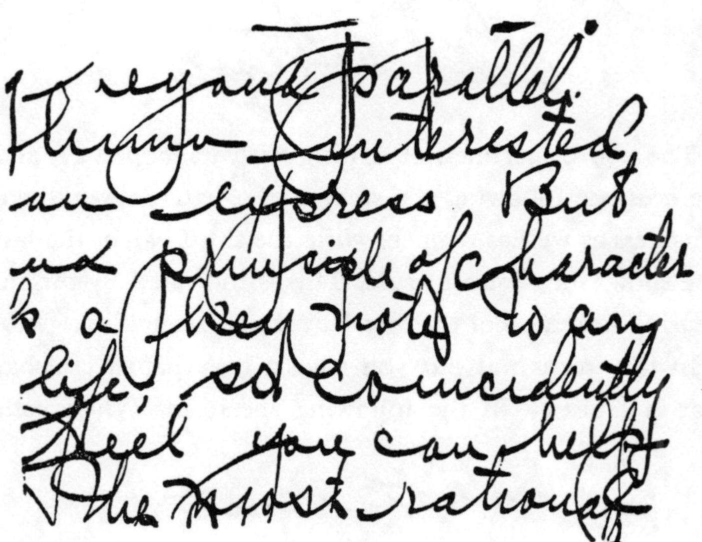

writing the lines run into the lines below as well as the lines above, indicating that the writer does not know what he wants. He is interested in everything, but specialized in nothing. He wants to travel, to see people, to have them do as he wishes. He is persistent, energetic in a wasteful sort of way, ready at any time to burst out into an angry demonstration, saying the most hateful things.

The above specimen of writing with its looped *t's*, and the crossbar following the stem of the letter, reveals sensitiveness as well as temper, while the third bar in the last line shows the desire to rule. This is indicated by the increasing heaviness of the crossbar, which resembles a club.

In the words *not put* you have a dish-shaped crossbar that is repeated in the following specimen. When your

writer crosses his *t's* with such a stroke his interests are shallow.

Even when you find evidence of keen or rapid thinking, the basinlike cross for the *t's* is undeniable evidence of shallowness of purpose and effort, as evidenced in the

specimen above. Such a writer may have many charming qualities, but when difficulties occur he will have a ready and possibly plausible excuse for not making a real effort to win.

On the other hand, crossbars that turn downward, as in the above, something like bars bent over a rail, indicate a very important trait that is directly opposite from shallowness. Such down-curved bars mean self-control or self-mastery. Very often you will find it in writing where you may least expect it, but no matter where it is you may know that that writer has at some time or another set about mastering habit, or gaining self-control, and this bowed crossbar is an expression of the will that has been used, and the self-mastery gained.

It is strikingly present, and combined with tenacity in the final hook, in the signature of the famous Alfred E. Smith, master politician, and famous example of a poor boy who made good. When Mr. Smith submitted his

writing for examination this was the first trait I noticed, and as you can see for yourself it is one of the strongest.

Those frequent breaks between letters revealed the strong musical sense and appreciation that must have made his heart beat faster when he heard *On the Side-walks of New York* so often during his presidential campaign. His frankness is clearly shown in the wide-open *d*, and the curved *t*-bar with its record of self-control carries all of the enthusiasm of the "happy warrior."

You may many times find handwritings that seem to be strangely contradictory. That is, the revelation of the writing may be so different from the actual life of the writer that you will feel that grapho-analysis has failed you completely. Do not worry. It has not done anything of the kind, and you will be merely discovering a truth that is all too tragically true. Too many people do not do the thing for which they have greatest natural talent, or do it very late in life. Almost thirty years ago a young physical director in a boys' school just out of New York City wrote to me. He sent along some photographs portraying a marvelous physical development.

That was my first acquaintance on paper with Earle Liederman, who was posing for artists and for magazine

illustrators. He was a great physical director, and undoubtedly his friends thought of him only as a physical training expert. His writing told a different story. It revealed a combination of musical interpretation and a strong literary strain. It was so clearly expressed that I put Earle Liederman down as a poet at heart if not in reality. His life seemingly contradicted the findings from his writing, but handwriting does not lie nor deceive, so when I needed an illustration for poetical ability I chose Liederman's writing, although so far as I knew he was interested solely in body building. I published the specimen and my comments, however, and here comes the most interesting part of the story, a sort of climax after many years. My first report was not submitted to Liederman. He was not influenced to take up poetry by anything I wrote or said. His handwriting revealed his talent for literary activity and for music, and the two together meant poetry. After several years I received a letter saying that he finished the manuscript of a book of poems. Almost forty years ago his handwriting showed that he could and should write poetry, and now he is fulfilling those indications. It took a long time, but he is doing the thing he has talent for doing.

I have brought the Liederman writing in here not only because of this interesting incident, but because of the way he crosses his *t's*, showing a fine sense of wit or sarcasm, depending upon his mood and circumstances. The crossbar in *best* starts with a thick head and runs down to a fine point, which is always an indication of satire, or wit, just as surely as the breaks between the letters show musical feeling, or the Greek *e* indicates a strong literary sense. Liederman had this talent and eventually he found it. Grapho-analysis finds the truth, even though it may not manifest itself for years.

The next bit of writing shows practical thinking, although Isabel Hornibrook wrote adventure books for boys. She was a practical thinker as she wrote these two lines, and being a practical thinker as she wrote, she was naturally a practical thinker in everyday living. I say this because many of my clients have raised the question

Yours very truly,
Isabel Hornibrook

whether writing one day will not be different from writing another day, and so fail to reflect the personality of the writer. There can be only one answer. Mental habits become established. Character traits are not a passing fancy. These mental habits, these established traits of character, show in the handwriting just as this woman showed her practical thinking in her life. Even if writers change the style of their letters, the fixed habits will remain and show in the writing.

You will find the *t*-bar in this specimen neither too high nor crowded down onto the writing itself. Miss Hornibrook shows by the placing of this single *t*-bar that she could see the opportunities of the future but did not forget the responsibilities accompanying them. On the other hand, these lines, written by a school boy, show doubt about the future. He crowds his crossbars down. He lacks vision and faith in himself. He is self-conscious, doubtful, but capable of growing stronger and more self-reliant. The crossbars are strong even if they are crowded on to the tops of the small letters. The boy procrastinates now but it is more the procrastination of doubt than that of laziness. He will improve throughout his life. His

nice book, and many
ks for it. it was just
I wanted or needed

d-stems are high, and his *f* in *for* is tied, showing persistence.

As you check the various strokes in this boy's writing, you will find from his *a's* that he is frank; in exactly the same way other strokes, curves, or hooks add their bit to the picture. Each must be taken into consideration in making up the exact picture of any given writer. This boy lived in the country. He had raised a prize-winning calf. He had found desired but unexpected success. Life was big and strange and wonderful, and the boy was self-conscious, more or less puzzled by having his picture in the papers, and having famous men congratulate him. His *t*-bars show lack of vision, but his *d*-stem is tall. He had pride, so that in spite of his apparent lack of ambition there is a good reason to hope that his pride and will power together cause him to set his goal far ahead. After all, this is one of the first benefits this boy could get from a grapho-analysis. It is one of the first benefits you too can get. You know definitely your shortcomings or your weaknesses, and you have a new vision of the worthwhile qualities you have with which to build a life.

As you study some of the famous handwriting in this book, and as you meet men and women whom you think you know very well, you will frequently find *t's* and *t*-bars revealing unsuspected traits. For example, when you find the *t*-stem made like a wigwam you can know the writer is stubborn. This inverted *t* may be in the body of the word, or at the finish, but if it is there, the writer is going to show stubborn streaks that will amaze you, if you have to deal with him. Stubbornness is not an uncommon trait, and a great many stubborn people insist that they are merely being determined. Possibly, but as you find these wigwam *t's* keep in mind that sincere belief is not stubbornness, but will show in strong will or great determination. It is the man or woman who refuses to give a point, even when wrong, who is stubborn. It is refusal to consider, to weigh, or give thought to any other angle of a situation. This is stubbornness and it shows in the handwriting.

In this specimen we have the writing of a stubborn man. He is stubborn, and he is also weak-willed, as you will discover when you study the crossbars of the *t's*.

He has judgment, but his stubbornness is stronger than his judgment and he lacks the will to be master of himself, or to overcome the negative stubbornness.

Summarizing this chapter into simple rules you will find that you have uncovered some exceedingly important character labels. Each rule has been tested innumerable times, not only in my own use of grapho-analysis but by business executives, teachers, professional people generally, and homemakers, too. They were taught to test each rule before they accepted it, and I pass this advice on to you. If you know by actual use that a rule stands up you do not have to depend upon what you have read in this book. You will know, and know that you know.

Now for the rules:

1. A *t* that is tied in a knot or with a knot reveals persistence. It may be in the body of a word or the last *t* but if it is tied it is evidence that the writer does not admit defeat.

2. A looped *t* is a sensitive *t*. The larger the loop the greater the sensitiveness of the writer.

3. A *t*-bar written above the stem reveals a habit of

building air castles; visionary, impractical, if the bar is light and short. If the bar is thick the writer has definite purposes, no matter how visionary they may seem. The thickness of the bar is important.

4. A light, short bar above the *t*-stem shows a dreamy disposition with little interest in making those dreams come true.

5. A long *t*-bar indicates enthusiasm. The longer the bar the greater the enthusiasm. When the bar is thick rather than light the enthusiasm is backed up by will power, and the enthusiasm will be energetically expressed.

6. A *t*-bar slanting downward from left to right has a value depending entirely upon the shape of the bar. When it is made like a knife blade, the writer will be domineering. When made equally heavy from start to finish, the writer will not domineer, but will dominate.

7. A thick blot or arrow shows temper if written after the *t*-stem.

8. A dish-shaped or crescent crossbar for the *t*-stem indicates a superficial nature, regardless of how rapid or keen a thinker the writer may seem to be.

9. A crossbar that is bent downward or like an inverted dish shows the use of will-power to gain self-control. Such a writer has earnestly attempted and to some degree has mastered some fault or weakness.

10. A crossbar made thick at the beginning, and ending in a thin knifelike edge reveals wit or sarcasm.

11. A crossbar that is well balanced, neither too high nor crowded down upon the tops of small letters, shows a practical nature.

12. A crossbar written far down on the *t*-stem indicates lack of purpose, absence of the adventurous spirit of reaching out to accomplish all possible.

13. A crossbar that is written back of the *t*-stem is evidence of procrastination. If the bar is light there will be little will power to overcome the trait, even when the writer realizes its existence.

14. A *t*-bar slanted upward, if made with a forward movement, from left to right, indicates an optimistic nature. However, such bars are usually from right to left and slanted downward. For this reason it is necessary to study the thickness of the stroke in making an estimate of its value.

15. When the last stroke of the *t*-stem extends through the base line of writing, it will be found to be thicker at the finish. This indicates a habit of thinking in terms of blunt emphasis. Such writer's opinions are final.

16. A *t*-stem written like a wigwam shows stubbornness, regardless of whether it occurs in the body or at the end of a word.

These sixteen rules are simple. Apply them to some of

the most famous handwritings and you will learn unexpected facts about the greatest people. Use them in analyzing your own handwriting, or that of your friends, and you may find yourself correcting earlier impressions, calling traits of character by their right names, and gaining a new understanding of those who have puzzled you. Very often *t's* and what they tell cover points that even honest biographers miss or do not dare to tell.

CHAPTER VII

AN EXPERIENCE YOU CAN DUPLICATE

BE yourself. At least do not try to be someone else, for you will find it exceedingly difficult at first, and eventually you will learn that it is impossible. You have certain mental habits, certain qualities of character which you have developed as you have grown older, and these qualities are yours. They do not belong to anyone but yourself, and you cannot adjust yourself to an assumed personality without destroying your own individuality.

It is true that you may find from an analysis of your own handwriting that you have certain traits which you wish to control or overcome. You may find that you are lacking in other traits and you may wish to develop these. All of this is entirely possible and is one of the direct benefits you derive from learning the truth about yourself from your handwriting. Any such self-control or guidance, however, is very much different from trying to assume an entirely new personality, with foreign traits of character. Such an effort sets up a conflict between the old and established habits, and the new and self-imposed ones that may easily be destructive to the nervous system, so that your new individuality will be a jittery, uncertain affectation, rather than real character.

In making these statements, I am drawing not only on simple reasoning but on many experiences, the most striking of which occurred in connection with the writing of a popular mystery novel. A year before he started active work on *The Matilda Hunter Murder*, the author, Harry Stephen Keeler, whose Chinese brush writing you will find in Chapter XI, wrote to me:

"I am temporarily stuck in a plot where I need a little grapho-analysis assistance. That is, I need to motivate the belief in the innocence of a young man, by an investigator, in spite of the existence of a number of damning factors against him, pointing him out to be the cold-blooded murderer of his aunt, as well as one who has apparently worked out a very *methodical* crime by which to get the sum of $2,000.00 in life insurance. Therefore I wonder if it is possible for you to provide me with a synthetic or artificial signature which would show the following points somewhat artificially or exaggeratedly brought out, i.e.:

" (a) That the writer would not be a *cold-blooded* murderer.

" (b) That his murder, if he did commit one, *would not be carefully planned out in all its details.*

" (c) That he does not particularly care for money,—per se.

" (d) That he has a strain of latent jealousy which can make him construe very fantastically things involving his lady love, and that therefore a jealousy murder is the only one in which he could possibly participate.

" (e) Outside of this the young man is about 25, inclined to business and drafting board experience or designing work, with general interests and no complexes, just a 'healthy hero' such as graces our modern fiction.

"If it is not possible at all to get the actual signature, then I would content myself with the verbal description of the points in such a character, as detailed from the mouth of one of the characters. The signature of the young man is 'Jeremy Evans.' "

These are rather simple requirements as you read them, but check them over and they are not so easy. Then try to write them and you will see why I say that you cannot become a new personality without terrific nervous strain and consequent upset.

1. In the first place, Jeremy Evans had to show his emotions quickly. He could not be cool and self-possessed. His writing had to slant well forward in order not to indicate cool self-possession. Only an impulsive character would

commit a crime on the spur of the moment in response to jealous excitement.

2. He had to be emotionally free enough to act without inhibitions. Some intensely emotional characters might commit a murder except for overpowering fear or caution. Jeremy Evans had to be free from such qualities.

3. He had to show in his handwriting lack of interest in getting or keeping money. He could be neither grasping nor possessed of a sense of thrift that would inspire him to accumulate by saving. He might want money, he might be a good spender, but neither of these traits of character could be strong enough to influence him greatly.

4. He had to be a fairly good mixer to avoid buried complexes. He had to have general interests aside from his drafting or designing.

5. Jeremy Evans had to think with the live activity of twenty-five and had to show that he had been trained to think. He had to be both a rapid thinker to meet business requirements, have something of an investigative nature, with the slant of the man who wants to learn, and also analyze. He had to become suspicious through discovery and analysis to qualify on the jealousy, for people are not jealous unless they are also suspicious. He would have to be capable of sharp resentment of imposition to arouse intense emotional reactions sufficient to commit a serious crime.

6. Finally, he would have to meet the technical requirement of revealing the engineering or architectural training in his signature, in order to fulfill Mr. Keeler's requirements.

This signature

is the one I worked out for the murder mystery. It is reproduced here because, although it contains only eleven letters, it took all of one afternoon to write it smoothly and naturally. It had the speed of execution that the fictitious Jeremy might have used if he had been a living, breathing man. That was what Mr. Keeler wanted, a Jeremy Evans to write like a real man, and in order to do this I had to subordinate my own mental habits, my own individuality, and for the time being assume all the qualities Jeremy Evans was supposed to possess.

It was necessary first to draw the signature, putting into the letter combinations all of the qualities necessary for Jeremy's personality and ability. Then I retraced the drawn outlines until my hand followed the letters automatically. At first I missed one trait or another. The exact mental procedure which characterized Jeremy was not my own mental plan, and my personal traits of character kept intruding themselves on Jeremy's personality. Just as I felt sure I could write Jeremy's signature easily, I would find that I was putting something of myself into the writing, and that something was contrary to some trait Jeremy simply had to possess to make Mr. Keeler's story come out right.

It may look easy enough but not until you try to build yourself into a new personality by writing a handwriting to fit such a personality can you know how fatiguing my task became after the first hour or two.

At this point, before going into the Jeremy Evans signature in more detail, let me make one suggestion to you as the reader. If you are earnestly interested in grapho-analysis, you will find the next few paragraphs interesting because they contain a stroke-by-stroke analysis of the signature. My suggestion is that you study the following paragraphs most carefully, for in them you will find invaluable information which will help you in the simple tests which will come up a little later, and which you will enjoy making.

1. The capital *J* starts with a decidedly boxlike or inverted swing for the upper loop. This twist gives us the undercurrent of jealousy which you found in the small *b* in an earlier chapter. The lower half of the capital swings far out to the left, getting the slant for intense emotional expression.

2. The capital letter swings right, through the inner line, and joins with the *e*, indicating virility of the writer.

3. The small *e* gives a cultural slant which helps to provide the required character for a man with a "healthy hero" qualification.

4. The writing swings right, up to the *r*, which is broadened or flattened sufficiently to indicate an engineering turn of thought, though not creative talent.

5. Our *e* is merely normal for this character.

6. The small *m* written well separated, one section from the other, gives us the opposite from stingy, selfish or overly thrifty, thereby accomplishing the requirement of the writer's mental condition by building up a contrary trait. The tops of the two first curves are well rounded, supporting the architectural drafting board qualifications. The base-line joinings are *v*-shaped, indicating an analytical or possibly critical frame of mind when resentment or jealousy is aroused. The last curve of the *m* swings well forward, and as an inflexible stroke, coming to a sharp point, then coming down and around, making the only hook in the signature. This would have acquisitive value if it had been at the beginning of a word, but here it does not have such meaning. The *y* is made with sharp points and the loop comes down with a good forward slant. The loop is narrow but it is not a clannish loop; instead it

indicates a writer who will be careful about selecting friends, and without any signs of exaggerated imagination. The final flourish is strong to the very tip, indicating a nature sufficiently emphatic to escape the wishy-washy, and also utterly devoid of meanness or brutality.

7. The *Evans* is written with a capital that is free from any flourish or flash. Such a capital would be made by a writer who thinks directly and clearly. There is no such thing as a business hand, because some business men who show remarkable ability to develop commercial ideas write in one way, and others write in another. However, the plainness and directness of this capital indicates one who thinks clearly and sharply.

8. The *v* starts with a direct stroke, curved very slightly indeed. This might almost be counted as an inflexible stroke, with its indication of resentment toward imposition. The letter itself is well formed, and is sufficiently separated from the *a* that follows to show that there is no stinginess. The *a* is closed, but there are no loops, so that we cannot check the writer as more than normally reticent. He is not talkative nor is he deceitful. The *n* forms a rounded point in the first curve, comes directly down, then rushes forward in another direct swinging stroke that comes to a point, and immediately swings down to an *s* that is finished off with an emphatic tail.

9. There is resentment of imposition in this last name;

a sharply defined sense of criticism, which, because of the deep emotional expression, gives us a decidedly deep resentment of emotional impositions, which, as you naturally understand, is jealousy.

Attempt to work out a signature indicative of traits of character you do not have. If you are a mild-tempered person, include in the signature the sharp explosive *i*-dots that indicate a quick temper. Add stubbornness if you wish, provided you are easily led. If your will is not strong, include a heavy *t*-bar that will express certain strength of will.

Next try this Concentration Test. This test is one which I have given to hundreds of those who have studied grapho-analysis with me during the past years. It is based on the rule that the smaller the writing, the greater the concentration of the writer. You start the test by writing any ordinary sentence in your usual style and size of handwriting. Rewrite it, but make the writing smaller. Rewrite again, and make your third writing smaller than either the first or second. Continue rewriting the sentence, each time making the letters smaller than the preceding until you find that you cannot reduce the writing any more and still keep it legible.

When you have finished the test you will experience a sudden let-down in nervous tension. You will no longer be centering your efforts on a single purpose, and will not be concentrating as you were when you were straining in an effort to make each line smaller than its predecessor.

These experiments reveal very clearly the effect that altering your handwriting has on an ordinary individual.

One of the most striking illustrations of small hand-writings revealing concentration came to me from the

> When my legs grow weary at the end o
> the shadows till the break. of Eternity's morn, I want to b
> Silver and gold? Ah, No! To others
> such gifts must go. They were not intended for me and
> made in their pursuit. Neither do I envy those who have ι
> The riches I want to leave, kind friends
> enough to earn them, are unselfish thoughts and deeds su
> I wish to have gathered about me there at the dusk of 2
> that I did not break faith with duty as I passed along
> jewels of memory glittering with a real and a serving love
> If none can say of me . then that I wr
> political arena,· I will be satisfied to know that somewhere
> that I stooped to pull a thorn from his wounded . foot,
> a friend made by one out in the dark night of need.

prize winner in a "most unusual handwriting" contest. The writing itself was not unusual; that is, the formation of the letters was not remarkable, but the size of the writing made it stand out as a very unusual specimen. Further, the writer explained to me that she had always written this way, that it was not in any sense a pose or an effort made solely to win the contest.

You will find each letter is clear and distinct, although the strokes themselves are so fine that it is almost like reading small type.

This writing reveals all of the writer's characteristics in exactly the same way that it would if she wrote a larger hand. The only difference is that when a writer has the power of concentration such as this writer shows, that concentration affects every other characteristic. In writing revealing sarcasm and concentration, you would have a sharper degree of sarcasm because of the concentration of the writer on the expression of that trait. Such a writer would be possessed of a far sharper tongue as a result of her intensity of concentration. In exactly the same way those who have highly expressive emotional natures frequently become hysterical, not so much because of the strength of their emotional expression, but because their natural emotional expressions are intensified by the element of concentration. It is like centering the rays of the sun with a lens on a small circle. The sun is not any more powerful, but the concentration of the rays through the lens gives the added heat to start the blaze. It is concentration that causes the blaze, and it is the habit of concentration that intensifies every other trait of character which you may find in the handwriting of anyone who writes an extremely small hand.

The writing of Rafael Sabatini showed one of the finest examples of concentration. He centered all of his efforts

on the thing he was doing; while he worked, he worked, and when he played, he played. He was a best seller on two continents, not only because of his literary ability, and there is no doubt about his talent, but because he concentrated on that ability, using it to the fullest extent. This small specimen, part of a letter regarding the size of the specimen he submitted for analysis, showed great initiative, a practical rather than visionary mind, and a remarkable memory. There are frequent breaks between letters in a word, the certain sign of musical appreciation. The small *g* in the first line is a half-formed figure 8, indicating his literary ability. His rapidity of thought is registered clearly by the fine pointed *m's* and *n's*, which you cannot read without the aid of a magnifying glass.

One added principle of grapho-analysis is illustrated in better than ordinary style by the Sabatini writing. In the date line, the month of May is spelled with a printed capital. The *D* in the salutation is also a printed letter. Again, in the closing, the *Y* is almost identical with a printed letter; at the same time the signature has a printed capital *R*, and the *S* is as much printed as written. All of this is interesting and revealing, for when you have many printed capitals in a handwriting, it is certain evidence of the writer's artistic sense. It may be developed along literary lines, in sculpture, music, or in a generally cultural life, but it is positive that it will find expression in one way or another.

The small *m* and *n* are important, not only in the Sabatini writing, but wherever you find them. The Sabatini *m's* and *n's* are sharp-pointed, although in every other particular they are entirely different from the *m's* and *n's* in the specimen on the next page. But in both the Sabatini writing and in this specimen, the letters are made with sharp upper points rather than rounded upper curves. Such sharp points show comprehension, or the ability to think rapidly and form conclusions immediately.

On the other hand, in a writer who makes broad and well rounded *m's* and *n's,* as in the signature of Mary Main Neb, you have a slower, more scientific thinker who

forms conclusions only after deliberate thought. An excellent example of this type of *m* and *n* can be found in the writing of Charles P. Steinmetz, in Chapter IV. Capital *M* is merely the small letter *m* grown larger, and is significant in only one important particular. If the last section or curve is higher than the middle section, the writer is self-conscious. This is illustrated in the specimen above, which shows the formation of both the capital and small letter indicating self-consciousness.

CHAPTER VIII

OCCULTISTS HAVE THEIR SAY ON GRAPHO-ANALYSIS

"Just what," my clients have asked me many times, "do you think of palmistry, astrology, and numerology?"

My answer has always been, and probably always will be, that I do not know, because I am not an astrologer, a palmist, nor a numerologist. One of the popular writers on numerology, a woman whose keen intellect I admire, studied grapho-analysis with me. That woman still uses her grapho-analysis to aid her in much of what she does, and wrote me later, "I could not get on without this help." Other practicing astrologers and numerologists have learned grapho-analysis, and tell me they use it daily. All of this has to do with what these "ologies" think of grapho-analysis, rather than what I think of them. Two of the most interesting characters, however, in my many years of making personal analyses were exponents of astrology and palmistry.

It has been a good many years since Count Louis Hamon, or Cheiro, world-famous palmist, sent me his writing. Wonderful writing, overflowing with character, ability, vitality. Cheiro had just returned from Europe when he submitted his few lines of writing, and his report was made along with others on hand. I have rarely found such depth of color, such strong emotions, combined with balancing qualities, and I mentioned this fact in my report. For that matter Cheiro's analysis was just like any other, complete,

covering minor traits just as exactly as those of greater prominence. Imagine my surprise a few days later to find an autographed photograph and this letter in my mail.

"I have received today your analysis of my character from the sample of my handwriting submitted to you. I can only say that it is *most accurate* in even the smallest particular. In fact, fairness compels me to add that it it such a remarkable description of my disposition and character that it is absolutely uncanny in its truthfulness."

Grapho-analysis had again earned its place in the sun, which after all was the thing that counted. It was easy to understand the impulsive generosity of Cheiro's letter, but his handwriting said that impulsive or not, he would tell the truth.

About the same time Dr. Francis Rolt-Wheeler, author

of a great many popular books for boys, and for years a highly successful newspaper man, wrote me from Tunisia, North Africa, where he headed the Institut Astrologique de Carthage, devoted to astrological research and the training of astrologers.

His signature included here will give you an understanding of his pride, self-reliance, frankness, and scientific inclinations, the latter revealed by the small *r*. Naturally

to find such a person engaged in astrology was a favorable sign, because it seemed to me then as now that a man with as much personal integrity as revealed by Dr. Rolt-Wheeler would not participate in something which he thought was without value. When he studied grapho-analysis with me, he revealed these very traits so strongly that I know that, no matter what there is to the subject of astrology, the man at the head of the greatest school in the old world devoted to astrological research believed in the subject he taught.

Other palmists and astrologers have submitted their

writing to me during the years. Some have gained attention in their chosen fields while others have not, but these two men, each possibly the greatest in his field, impressed me by the intelligence revealed in the handwritings. They at least believed what they taught and practiced.

Of course grapho-analysis does not pretend to predict the future. Instead, it deals with what you are today and what you may become as the result of your present traits and inclinations. It is equally true that very many of my clients have insisted that grapho-analysis, indicating what they might become, actually foretold the future events. Grapho-analysis does nothing of the kind. It is not fortunetelling, but it is *analysis*. If you find a writer lacking in personal integrity, ruled by emotions, and by acquisitiveness, you can predict a potential criminal. Grapho-analysis does not imply that the writer *must be* a criminal, but merely reveals the individual, and shows the road he is traveling through life. Grapho-analysis, however, is not related to numerology, astrology, or palmistry, at least as far as I can learn from the leading exponents of these various systems, and in spite of the fact that Meredith Nicholson, the famous novelist wrote me: "My wife says you are right!" he said. "My birthday is December 9, and the astrologers 'got me' pretty well. I suppose they all get their stuff out of the same book!"

Mr. Nicholson erred in his belief. They do not get their

stuff from the same book, any more than Mr. Nicholson's own novels all come out of the same book as those of

Booth Tarkington or E. Phillips Oppenheim or Temple Bailey. Every writer has individuality, and palmistry is not related to astrology, or if it is, I am mistaken in my understanding of what the experts teach. Grapho-analysis is not related to any of these manifestations with which I am familiar.

Grapho-analysis is not psychic, although it reveals the psychic. An interesting experience with this trait came when James Oppenheim sent me his writing, and then took me to task rather sharply for not stressing his weaknesses. "They are glaring and they should be in my writing," he wrote, adding, "Your bull's-eye is about my musical gift. It lies in words—poetry. My collected volume *The Sea* was written, all but the first part of it, on a musical basis. Inspiration for one poem came through a dream where I heard bars of music which I turned into words or word sounds as best I could. I am a poet who has also

developed his thinking to the extent of becoming somewhat of a psychologist."

So, though Mr. Oppenheim felt I had not struck his
weaknesses, he revealed that the strongest single influence

in his make-up was expressed by his writing, i. e., his
psychic sense. He felt, he sensed the invisible, he touched
that which was not apparent, whereas his judgment of
personal faults was not after all an impartial judgment. As
I later explained to Father Abell of Loyola University in
New Orleans, there are very few actual weaknesses, but
very often excellent traits of character are badly used, and
so lose their place as assets and become liabilities.

It was interesting to find too that Mr. Oppenheim was

inclined to credit grapho-analysis with his own personal strong point, as he wrote, "I have sampled astrology, palm reading, all of them, and in every case I get some remarkable results. My astrologer and palm reader admitted, however, that they used intuition as well as science. Do you not do the same?"

You may have the same question. There is only one answer; "No." If grapho-analysis required a psychic sense then there would be no use for the rules I am giving in this book. You would have to merely worship and analyze at a distance. But you *can* learn these rules and you *can* apply them. Mr. Oppenheim's writing told the truth. He lived and breathed music. It was the very heart of him, and because it was revealed so clearly in his writing, he felt that what I did with grapho-analysis must have something mystic about it. He was not alone in this view.

Dr. Henry Van Dyke, famous for his *The Fourth Wise Man,* even went so far as to insist that I looked for his his-

tory in reference books. The great doctor did not realize that I did not recognize his name, that it did not mean anything to me. Even though I had read a collection of his stories I did not know whether the author was living or dead. His analysis had been made on the strength of what his writing revealed and was a center shot, for his handwriting had revealed that he was entirely analytical. He had to analyze bit by bit, and it was not reasonable to him that, a thousand miles away, I could take a dozen lines of his writing and reconstruct his personality.

Such doubt about grapho-analysis is quite natural in a keenly analytical writer, who after proving the merits of the subject, becomes a firm convert. Some of my best students have been accountants whose natural analytical ability had been emphasized by training. When they had analyzed the *why* of grapho-analysis, they saw its value. It has been not only exceedingly interesting but amazing as well that many of my earlier clients were convinced that I had a confederate who rushed out and gathered information about individual writers. Of course such a viewpoint overlooks the fact that thousands of specimens have been submitted unsigned.

You too will experience just such situations as you apply the rules which you find in this book. All the while, though, you will be merely using simple scientific rules that are in no way associated with the mystic.

All of this, however, is a very long way from the question of what I think of astrology, palmistry, or numerology, or for that matter anything occult. There are truths that the mind of man has not yet fathomed, and only a pedant will set himself up as denying a thing about which he knows nothing. I do not know anything about palmistry, numerology, and astrology. It has taken many years of research to establish positively and exactly the rules which you have in this book. That is, it has taken these years to answer my first question of why I swung my pen forward, making tails on my words. I have not had time for digging out facts for or against these other subjects, but I do know that when you find a long downstroke for the g repeated many times in a page of writing, that the writer has more than ordinary determination. I know this, and also know why it is true.

CHAPTER IX

GRAPHO-ANALYSIS SOLVES THE VALENTINO MYSTERY

Why was Rudolph Valentino a universal favorite? What was there about the man that made him loved, admired, not only while he lived, but after his death? Other motion-picture stars have lived, died, and been forgotten, but not Rudy. He is still a favorite. There is no question about it. His fans still hold his memory dear, keeping it alive with active Valentino clubs, and periodical revivals of Valentino films. What is the explanation for such permanent fame?

Motion-picture magazine and film editors have asked these questions. The fans themselves have asked them. What was it Rudolph Valentino possessed that other actors have not had, which gave him a permanent place in the hall of motion-picture fame? You may have considered the same question. If so, here is the answer, taken from Valentino's own handwriting. It was there that he revealed himself as he did in no other way. Every stroke of his writing shows the man, what he was, and what he might have become.

Hours piled upon Hours of sheer
beauty and rest .... Now and
then some little thing of irritation
to prove to me that I am not apart
from the world of material troubles..

It was shortly after World War I, when I was editing a popular boys' magazine, that I first saw Valentino's writing. He submitted a feature about the value of youthful body building, and posed for a number of illustrations.

His writing struck me because it was unusual; in fact it was such a revealing and at the same time complicated writing that I laid it aside so that I might study it further, and might follow out his channel of thinking.

Valentino was a complicated and at the same time exceedingly simple personality. He had no deep, dark secrets although his life in itself became an unsolved secret. Rudolph Valentino was first of all a puzzle. Undoubtedly he was one even to himself. He loved beauty more than any other one thing in life. He wanted to possess it, to have it, to make it his own. He was not ambitious in the usual sense of the word, and he was not vain for mere vanity's sake. It is true he was proud. He would not sully his name nor his pride for anything. His handwriting reveals this pride in the tall, dignified *d* stems. It is pride, but not false pride. His personal integrity was above reproach. Rudolph Valentino was worth knowing for this single trait alone.

It was one of the first things I saw when I examined his handwriting for the first time. The next thing outstanding was the utter loneliness of the man. Look at his small *g* and you will find the narrow loop showing his isolation. Rudolph Valentino did not let anyone know him; he simply could not do it. His life was something he did not understand, and he could not share it with others. When you find a writer who makes his small *g* loops so narrow that the loop itself is closed, you may be sure that the writer lives unto himself.

In this he was deceitful, in that he always tried to create an impression to cover up something which even he, within himself, did not understand. He did not want to deceive others in order to hurt them, but to cover up his own personality which he could not solve.

In spite of this, Valentino wanted love and understanding. He wanted them more than life itself. It is this hopeless longing for love that created the mystery of his personality, and it is this very mystery that holds his followers today. It was the longing for beauty, for love that he could not have that produced the spiritual atmosphere so many of his admirers have found in his acting.

Study his handwriting and you will find repeated breaks between letters; not in the letters themselves, but between letters. You find it in his *Irri-tati-on,* again in *f-rom,* in *w-orld,* and in *materi-al.* These are not merely pen lifts, but are a reflection of the psychic or musical qualities of the mind that guided the pen. It is positive evidence that at heart Valentino was a musician, with a nature that comprehends music as only a master musician understands it.

Through all of his loneliness, and his worldly success, he was still a self-conscious young fellow, never quite aware of the material success he had achieved. Startled by it, he did not see in his earnings or his fame a chance to strut and preen himself. He was just a lad who loved beauty and music, but who had made a tremendous success which puzzled him and made him even more self-conscious. Rudolph Valentino was an artist, not merely a motion-picture performer who won fame and a tremendous salary. His rewards puzzled him, just as life itself puzzled him. He was applauded and praised, and he was still more perplexed by it all.

He loved flowers. He loved a beautiful body. He would have loved to grow green things, trees, plants, and shrubs. He would have loved to rise with the birds, work with growing things, and then in the cool of the evenings, sing his song of life and happiness. That was the famous Rudy as he revealed himself to me in his first specimen of handwriting. He did not change. The specimen reproduced at the head of this chapter, written shortly before his death, shows the same qualities. He was still the same old Rudy who wrote articles for me years before.

But there is more in this writing. There is decay, the cry of the soul worn sick with longing for the things he could not have. Not wealth, nor huge motor cars, nor his name in bright lights, but the woods and the trees and companionship which he could not find. All of these things meant so much to the young actor and they were so very far away from him during the days of his success. Even the throngs who admired him, who were Valentino fans, were so far away from him. They thought of him as a great actor, but not as a human being, and it was this last that increased the loneliness of the boy grown into manhood. Rudolph Valentino was a great actor, but he was a great actor second, and a great but puzzled personality first.

Hollywood has given me so many striking personalities, men and women who have possessed rare talent apart from any showing they made in pictures. Possibly next to Valentino was Ramon Novarro, who, had he remained active in pictures, would have made as great a name for himself as Valentino. I shall never forget the circumstances of my first examination of Novarro's writing.

I knew of him as an actor. That was all, but two of my assistants were loud in his praise. However, I had no thought of analyzing his writing until one afternoon, after completing a large number of reports for actors in Hollywood, we were discussing them both as personalities and as performers. I remember that I was enlarging upon the marvelous courage and determination of Irene Rich, as shown by her writing. Her specimen had been brief, but in the face of its paucity of strokes I had found great self-reliance, courage, as well as simplicity of living and tastes.

I remember that I commented that if more women, left in serious straits with children to support, would face life with the courage Miss Rich revealed in her writing, the world would have fewer children developing into failures. Then one of my assistants said that it would be interesting to examine the handwriting of Ramon Novarro. I remember that she emphasized this as though it would be a great experience, and that is what it proved to be. Within a week Novarro's writing was submitted to me. Only a few lines, but such lines! Filled with talent. Filled and overflowing, but not with talent for the stage. Talent for music. He was thinking, breathing, living rhythm. Every line of his writing revealed it along with a wonderful tone and color sense. It was amazing, for it is rare that you find such distinctive ability for a new field of effort in the writing of someone who has already achieved success in one field. Novarro was living music, even as Valentino felt it. There was one marked difference between the two men, and between the two handwritings. Valentino was lonely, confused, questioning, longing for that which he did not have. Ramon Novarro was shy, timid, but sure of himself in spite of his timidity. He was self-reliant, and at peace with himself. He knew what it was that he wanted, and his writing showed the strength of character to bring his ambitions to a head. Valentino was a servant to the demands made upon him, while Novarro knew within himself that he was master of his own fate.

That is how I first became familiar with Novarro, but I prepared his report with considerable hesitation. There are many persons of great ability who have won success, who long for something different, but who still resent being told that they have not found themselves, that their greatest talents have not been used. Not Ramon Novarro, however. Almost at once he sent back word expressing his appreciation and approval. More than this, he said he was satisfied that I had helped him.

"No man knows much about himself," he wrote, "but what little I do know of myself I found that you had accurately gauged from my handwriting. Your analysis as a whole has encouraged me very much because it gives me hope that I may fulfill several cherished wishes. I think that the science is indeed a valuable one."

Ramón Novarro.

Later, when Novarro withdrew from the screen, his followers were puzzled and amazed, but they had not seen his handwriting. If they had, they would have known the truth revealed by his writing, that kleig lights, newspaper stories of success, and a huge salary were not all of life for him. He may have taken a lesson from Valentino. At least he refused to permit himself to be dragged into the black loneliness and make-believe that Rudy suffered. I believe that his one desire was to devote himself to the art of living when he retired from the screen. His writing showed me his courage.

This was being merely natural, for Novarro's writing contained the same thin loops in the *g's* and *y's* that were so prominent in Valentino's. They were both clannish at heart, both longing for a few intimate friends, but lacking the desire to be mere good fellows or good mixers. Novarro had the courage to quit and be himself before it was too late. He had earned money, and fame enough; and he wanted quiet, seclusion, and happiness. His handwriting proved to me that he had the courage to retire while he was still popular.

Speaking of courage among motion-picture people however, there are two women who stand out above all others. The first of these is Louise Fazenda, the great comedienne, who began in early picture days, and carried on into the days of talking pictures. Even now she plays occasional parts, as she will probably do for years to come. Time and again Miss Fazenda sent me her writing, and just as often wrote of her delight in the accuracy of the reports, and the benefit she received from them. Her letters were always as brimful of enthusiasm as this one:

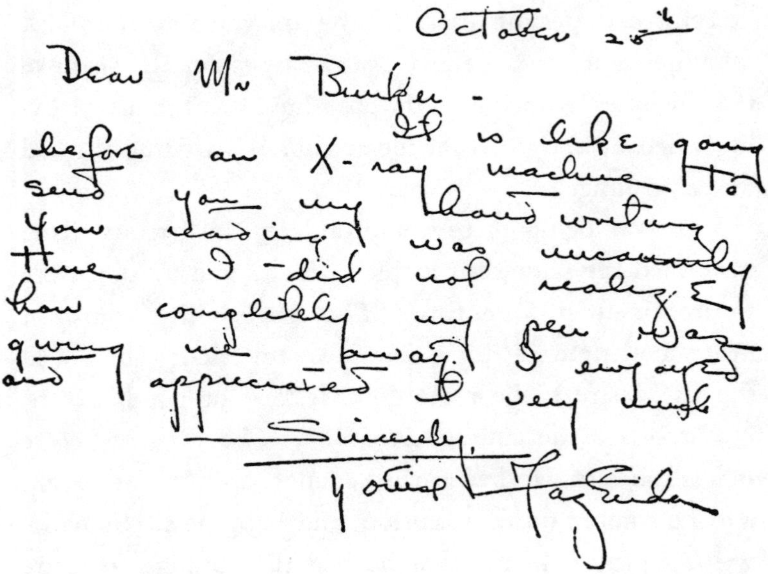
October 20th

Dear Mr Bunker -

It is like going before an X-ray machine to send you my handwriting. Your reading was uncannily true. I did not realize how completely my pen was giving me away. I enjoyed and appreciated it very much.

Sincerely,

Yours Louise Fazenda

Pen-written, this letter does exactly what Miss Fazenda's writing always does. It reveals her optimism, in the long crossbars of her *t's*. It shows her undying determination in the long downstrokes of her *y's* and *g's*. Her sensitiveness is as plain as it can be in her very large *d* and *t* stems. The long sweeping strokes of the crossbar over the *L* in *Louise* and the same sweeping upward stroke in crossing the capital *F* are there to reveal her hopefulness, and belief that things will be better in the future. There is keen comprehension in the sharp points of the *n* and *m* and great decisiveness in the blunt final stroke of many of her words. Her writing is revealing; it shows the real Fazenda which explains my admiration for her personality. I have never seen her, but I know that in spite of great sensitiveness she has never given up nor been on the verge of doing so. Instead she carries on, head up, no matter how disappointed she may be. She has courage.

It was the same with Marie Dressler, "grand old woman" of the screen. It was during the dark days of the depression that I found a thick blue envelope in my mail. Marie Dressler wanted to know what, if anything, her handwriting revealed. It was unusual writing, but Marie Dressler was an unusual personality, a rare combination of keen intelligence and judgment.

Marie Dressler's signature, reproduced here, reveals a mature woman, who as a girl was extremely self-conscious,

one who might have hidden behind her mother's apron and excused herself from success by saying she could not face people. Not Marie Dressler. Her self-consciousness in her mature writing is still as plain as it can be, but that signature shows courage and self-reliance. The way she tied the double *ss* showed her persistence. Marie Dressler simply could not admit defeat. She would not give in to failure. No matter what came along, no matter how many bitter disappointments and disillusionments she had to meet, she would not go down. She would get up and battle them and carry on, a winner. Her personal history as told by others shows all of these traits, but Marie wrote the story in the signature.

I made her report. I pointed out her weaknesses, and I tried to avoid enlarging on the marvelous courage of the writer. All the time, though, I felt as if I were working on a master drawing, each sentence a necessary part of the picture. I had admired Miss Dressler in her screen presentations as a great artist, but after I made that report, I knew her as a greater woman than an artist. One of my most prized possessions today is a beautifully autographed photograph which the great Marie gave me a few days after her report was delivered.

Hollywood has provided many unusual personalities. Some of them have been openly skeptical, and others have looked on grapho-analysis as a sort of fortunetelling, at least until they had their own intimate reports. Almost all have expressed amazement at the way in which even a few of their pen strokes have revealed their most personal habits.

As in the case of Valentino, my first examination of Conrad Nagel's writing was made as a result of correspondence about other matters, but that report was for my own use. It was not until he reached stardom that he sent me his writing for analysis. The specimen came, the report was made, and forwarded to the actor, and I gave the matter no more thought until he wrote to me again. While making the report, his writing had impressed me by the love of responsibility it revealed in the large circles at the beginning of his capital *M's* and *N's*.

"Location work has caused me to neglect my correspondence for over two months. I enjoyed very much the analysis which you sent, and both Mrs. Nagel and I consider it quite uncanny that without knowing me you can so thoroughly analyze my character, and my likes and dislikes, merely from my rather illegible signature. I imagine that yours must be a fascinating work."

Mr. Nagel was right. All I ever had of his writing was his signature. My own analysis, made for myself years before, was analyzed from a signature, and when he asked for his report he merely signed his name, but that signature revealed him intimately.

On the other hand, many of the movie people have written letters, such as the one from Richard Arlen. If you will study the flourishes in the capital *M's* and *N's,* you will find they reveal a fine sense of humor. Contrast them with

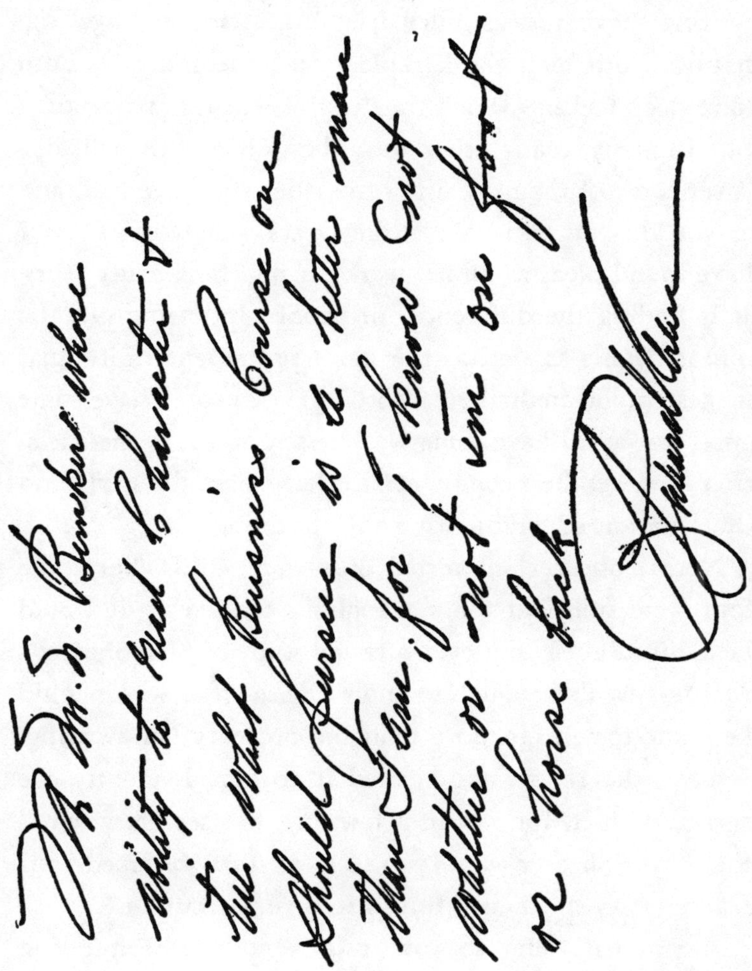

the large circles in Conrad Nagel's writing and you discover a decided difference in the two men. The Arlen

writing shows just as much friendliness as the Nagel signature. Both men think rapidly and energetically. Both have deep feelings which they express clearly and readily, but in many, many other ways they differ. You will discover some of them by using the rules you have had, and as you do you will enjoy using grapho-analysis just as I have found pleasure in my work during these many years. It is finding the differences in people, following out the minor details as well as the more prominent traits, that makes grapho-analysis so absorbing. All people have some good just as all have some weaknesses, and it is the variation of the endless combinations that makes the study and examination of handwriting so interesting.

Norma Shearer submitted only four words, but those four were sufficient for her analysis. Ordinarily it would be a difficult task, but even a casual study of Miss Shearer's writing revealed enough to know that the four words could be made to tell far more than the ordinary handwriting. I made the report and mailed it to her. Evidently she agreed with it, for within a few days her secretary wired that "Miss Shearer wants you to know that she liked your reading very much and thinks it is very accurate."

If you will refer to your own Emotional Expression chart you will discover that Miss Shearer's life is ruled by sound judgment, but that she possesses real depth of feeling. Her *m's* show that her mind works with the rapidity of lightning. She forms conclusions rapidly, but those conclusions are directed by her judgment and, therefore, are sound. She possesses strong cultural qualities which are revealed by the breaks between letters coupled with the Greek *E* which she uses for the small letter. Her sense of color, tone, and flavor are good, so that she naturally selects attractive apparel, harmonious surroundings, and will appreciate music or other tones.

Altogether it is a very interesting handwriting, and quite naturally reveals an equally interesting personality. On the other hand, after you have studied Miss Shearer's writing you will find a much different, but no less interesting study by referring to the note from Warner Baxter on page 57. Here the slant of the writing is far forward. Just how much, you can easily determine for yourself by using your own Emotional Expression chart. Notice that the crossbar on the *t* in *Baxter* is very long, while under the signature there is another sweeping stroke that slants upward. The long, well-rounded *y* loops are anything but clannish, while the slant of the writing reveals the impulsive friendliness of the writer.

Ben Blue's request for his own analysis was much different. In this writing you find a well-developed forward

slant, and frequent breaks between the letters. In his word *reactions* there are four distinct breaks, each adding their weight to the evidence that the comedian loves music, not merely because it is tuneful but because he understands or gets the feel of the intangible aspect of music. If you study his writing carefully you will find as I did the signs of self-consciousness, the frankness, and the diplomacy, all of which are written into these few lines.

Very often, as I have said, those who have submitted their writing for analysis have seemed anxious to see how few of their pen strokes they could submit and still discover the truth about themselves, and whether handwriting tells those truths. Joel McCrea did not write a letter, he sent nothing but his signature. Starting with the large loop or circle before the *M*, you will find just as I did that Joel McCrea likes responsibility. He intends to make good,

to do a better job tomorrow than he did yesterday. The short upward stroke under the *Mc* reveals inflexible self-reliance, and the *e* in *Joel* showed me the literary inclinations you will find for yourself if you use your rules.

It is not necessary for me to go ahead with the analysis, for if you have studied rules enough to follow what we have uncovered in this signature you have knowledge enough to go ahead and make a very interesting analysis for yourself. You can discover Joel McCrea's strong color sense, and preference for deep, rich tones, his ability to make decisions, and his ability to keep things to himself. Possibly you will find much more, just as I did, so that even though the actor had been chary about the amount of writing he gave me on which to work, he was open and frank enough in his approval. "I must say," he wrote, "that your analysis is very good—so good in fact that I can hardly believe you could do so well without knowing me." Of course he overlooked the single fact that I did know him; that I knew his innermost desires, longings, his habits, all from his handwriting, and that this knowledge was much more reliable than if I had listened to his friends or had met and talked with him. What others say is likely to be biased, while the things you say in your writing is entirely a reflection of *you*.

In the past very many of my students have asked me not to analyze a specimen for them, but let them make their own analyses. You may feel the same way, so I have selected three specimens which are each sufficiently interesting to provide you with some fascinating revelations. In each case the amount of writing selected for your study is the equal of the amount furnished for the analysis made for the writer.

John Boles merely gave me his signature, although later he said he enjoyed the way in which his report pointed out his faults and virtues.

This request from Herbert Mundin is the one from which his report was made.

Charles Butterworth's letter is fully as long as his first specimen. Therefore I feel fully justified in saying, "Reader, these are yours. Take them away. Do with them as you

will, for they are worth studying, and you can get the truths they reveal for yourself just as well as if I were to point them out to you. Learn the truths revealed by these specimens of writing and you will know the writers. Forget what you have heard about them, and get at the intimate facts as they are revealed by the writing of each."

CHAPTER X

TESTIMONY ON A FAMOUS RANSOM NOTE

"WHAT about the Lindbergh case?" "What do you think of Hauptmann?" and "Do you think we shall hear anything more about it?"

Visitors ask the questions. Correspondents, submitting handwriting from the Orient, from the South Sea Islands, from the most distant points, as well as from every state in the Union and every Province in Canada ask just such questions. Those who came to me for a personal analysis in order to straighten out a family difficulty or make a choice in vocations have frequently stopped in the middle of the discussion to ask, "What do you think about the Lindbergh case?" They overlook the point that a graphoanalyst deals only in facts, and until those facts are available and sometimes after they are, he says nothing.

I did not take part in the trial. Some months before the case came up in Flemington, New Jersey, I sat in the private office of a New York man who was then and is today high in the penmanship field. He suggested that I contact the attorneys on one side or the other, adding that it looked as though there might be a "big show."

We discussed the matter, pro and con. My feeling about expert testimony is that it is not a matter of showmanship, but of science, and that no man can accept a questioned-document case of any kind until he has examined the documents and formed a conclusion for or against his possible client. I have never believed that any man living has a right to take money or participate in a show when lives are at stake. This very great authority on penmanship agreed with me, and I left his office with the definite decision that I would not have anything to do with a trial that was to attract all the activities of a side show.

An expert in any field who goes into any single case solely to win, and thereby earn a very large fee, seems to me to be failing in the fulfillment of his duty as an expert. Such a man might justify his conduct, but his opinion would still be prejudiced by his fee. This was my reasoning, supported by the association I had with L. C. Spencer, who was for many years one of the greatest questioned-document examiners in the South, if not in all of America. It was Mr. Spencer who published my first articles on handwriting, thereby influencing me to undertake the years of research to arrive at the principles of grapho-analysis, and to understand the *why* behind those principles.

His position on the matter of testimony seemed fair and just. A handwriting analyst, regardless of whether he devotes his time to identifying questioned documents or to analyzing character should be interested only in the truth, not in the fee, and not in providing a defense, but in getting at the facts. I felt this way about the Hauptmann-Lindbergh case, and I still hold that view. All of the published controversy since the trial and execution of the condemned man justify my having passed the entire matter by, especially in view of the fact that I had come in contact with the case many months before Bruno Hauptmann or anyone else was accused.

At the time, I was associated with a detective magazine published in Minneapolis, and the editor of that magazine gave me the opportunity to examine the material in this case that had come to his desk. I stopped over in the city for a few hours in order to visit the editorial offices on my return from a prolonged radio broadcasting session on southern stations. The editor had the photographs of the ransom notes on his desk and asked me to take them and give him an analysis of them, if possible reconstructing the physical appearance of the writer. In less than an hour, working steadily, I prepared the analysis that is reproduced here. It was published, and it still stands as a picture of the character who wrote the notes.

However, this does not mean that the man who wrote the note which I analyzed was guilty of the kidnaping. This writing indicates that if Hauptmann had been guilty

Handwriting Shows LINDY KILLER Will Talk

Says M. N. BUNKER
Noted Grapho-Analyst

Cruelly used to trick Colonel Lindbergh into believing his child safe, this letter is said to reveal garrulous characteristics that will make it impossible for the kidnaper to keep his secret.

ONE of the Lindbergh killer gang will talk. He can't keep silent.

This is shown with utmost clarity by the handwriting of the ransom notes to "Jafsie" resulting from the Bronx negotiations.

The writing is clearly that of a man who talks too much. It is shown from the very first line to the last. The writer is "gabby." He can't keep things to himself.

When he talks he will lie. He has done it many times, so many that he has developed an unconscious habit of misrepresentation. He has talked too much and has had to talk his way out of what he has already said.

His whole handwriting bears this out —for this is not his natural writing. Instead of writing with a fair degree of speed as he ordinarily would do he has dragged his pen across the paper, adopting the "push and pull" scheme that is found in a majority of forgeries committed by the beginner. He has tried to deceive by this method of writing, but instead has merely brought out more clearly traits of character that might otherwise have been less apparent. Here they are:

1. First he is a pessimist.

2. He is final. An opinion once formed will not be changed. A statement made will not be recanted. It is the spirit of "Me and God."

3. The writer has either played a musical instrument or has a well-grounded natural appreciation of music.

4. He eats too much or in other ways indulges his physical appetites.

5. He has no code of ethics. He does not care what the other fellow thinks, because his own way is right.

6. He will have few if any intimate friends. Is too critical—too likely to find fault, and too stubborn about giving in to attract people to him.

7. Finally, anything he might write or say would have all the chances of being untrue.

Grapho-Analysis does not give a picture of the physical make-up of the individual, but a man's mental habits are frequently reflected in his physical structure.

This man is likely to have a cold but not a penetrating eye. He will not be over normal height, and is likely to be decidedly less than normal height. Weight around 145 pounds. Will be found to wear down the heel of the right shoe. This is a common habit but in this case the wearing down of the heel is very decided, and may even cause the right shoe to slouch over.

Hair will be bristly and not dark. He is likely to have cold gray or green eyes. His mouth will have rather thick lips that close in a hard line, making them seem thinner at times.

May at some time have studied music or art, been disappointed, and developed his resentment of the advantage of others as a result of that experience. Without doubt there is a bitter grudge against either Colonel Lindbergh, some member of his family, or a class grudge against those who have won success or wealth.

There is plenty of evidence that the writer does not value his own life; that he is a fatalist. He took a chance—and with this fellow if the cards turn up wrong, it is a matter for a mere shrug of the shoulders. One life more or less does not matter—even if it is his own.

he would have talked freely. He would have become en-
tangled in his own stories, for the very wide open *a's* and
o's mean frankness or loquacity and the wider the opening
the greater the talkativeness. These letters are very wide
open, indicating the extreme of talkativeness or frankness.
Such a person could not keep a secret, certainly not a
secret of crime and sinister plotting. If Hauptmann wrote
these notes, or at least if he wrote the sample of handwriting which I was given to analyze, he did not commit
the crime, and did not know anything about it beyond
what he may have admitted. Too many men and women
showing these wide open vowels have talked themselves
into the chair, no matter how much iron nerve they had.
You can put it down as a hard and fast rule that such
wide-mouthed letters show talk without reason, a steady
flow of words, even when keeping still would be the wiser
course.

This is my only answer to the Hauptmann-Lindbergh
question. If Bruno Hauptmann had been guilty, his talkativeness would have led him to say so much that he would
have tied the rope around his own neck. If Hauptmann
wrote the note, he did not commit the crime. According
to all admitted records the man did not confess either to
Harold G. Hoffman, then governor of New Jersey, or to
any visitors. As governor, Hoffman had no interest what-
ever in the case except as chief executive of his state, and

he was determined to see that justice was done. He was praised and commended for his attitude in holding up Hauptmann's execution. This sample of his handwriting gives an exact estimate of Harold G. Hoffman, not only in regard to this particular case but toward any other problems he faced or may face in the future.

His writing shows Mr. Hoffman to be a man ruled by judgment, with great persistence. His thinking is instinc-

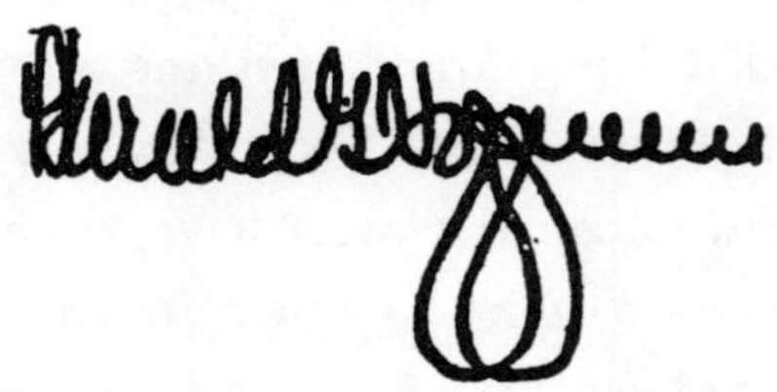

tive and very penetrating. He is fearless and entirely practical. The short upper loops of the *f* along with the very much longer lower loops reveal a man too practical to meddle in something unless his judgment satisfied him that it was the right thing to do. My judgment based on his handwriting is that Mr. Hoffman was not satisfied that justice was done in the case, and he had too much persistence to let go of his beliefs.

He may have had one eye on the public sentiment while discussing Hauptmann's trial, but there is nothing in his writing to reveal any such tendency, and experience has taught me that if he wanted applause it would show in his signature. In exactly the same way I arrive at my own conclusions that the case is not closed. During the trial of Bruno Hauptmann and since, various handwriting specimens have come into my possession for study. They have each told their own story, not of the criminal, but of the characters who participated in the tragic show at Flemington, and on the basis of these pictures it seems to me in the face of any opinion to the contrary, that the Lindbergh kidnaping case is not closed.

I am not a magician, and there is nothing more for me to work upon in saying that this case is not closed, than I had in saying that Charles "Pretty Boy" Floyd was a member of the murder party in the Kansas City Union Station Massacre in June 1933. At that time newspapers were quoting the police as satisfied that Floyd was not in Kansas City, nor a member of the murder party, yet Floyd's own writing gave him away.

Witnesses agreed and disagreed concerning identifications, until on June 20, the postal card reproduced here was mailed at Springfield, Missouri, and addressed to the Kansas City Police Department. On the face of that card in crude printing was the message, "I—Charles Floyd want it made known that I did not participate in the massacre of officers at Kansas City. Charles Floyd."

Was Floyd lying? Did he write the card? What was the truth? The newspaper reports said that the police accepted

Floyd's denial, but in spite of these statements, Lieut. Wm. A. Gordon, Identification Expert, sent the photostatic copy of Floyd's signature and of the front and back of the card to me. That signature said that Floyd would not tell the truth. It did not say that Floyd lied in this particular case, but it did say that when "Pretty Boy" went to the point of denying a thing, his denial would be false because he lacked the ability to tell the truth.

You can check his writing for yourself, and see how I arrived at my findings. The first *a* in *Chas.* represents a double loop even though the loop is broken on the inside of the letter. It is a deceitful letter. The capital *A* tells the same story. The *o* in *Floyd* has been circled around and tied, and the same thing appears in the *d*. Naturally a deceiver, when any emergency occurred the natural thing would be for Floyd to try to lie out of it.

That report had to stand in the face of popular doubt, and not until months later was there anything except the handwriting evidence to support the opinion. Then the FBI learned the truth. Floyd's handwriting had revealed him. He had lied.

It is this simple fact that the handwriting of an individual is more certain evidence than his sworn testimony may be, that brings me back to my original stand on the Hauptmann case. The man who stole Baby Lindbergh either did not write the ransom notes, or did not commit

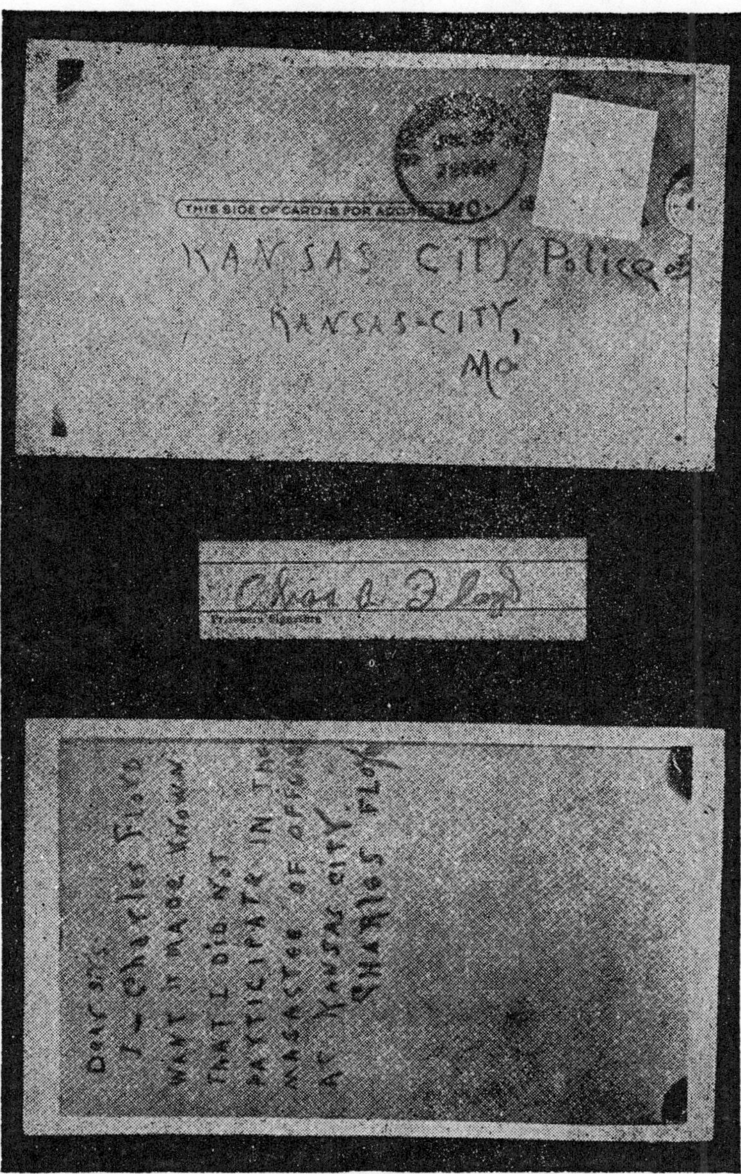

THIS SIDE OF CARD IS FOR ADDRESS
KANSAS CITY Police
KANSAS-CITY,
Mo.
Chas A Floyd
Prisoner's Signature
Dear Sirs
I—Charles Floyd
want it made known
that I did not
participate in the
Massacre of officers
at Kansas City.
Charles Floyd

the crime of kidnaping. If the man who wrote the note had been accused, he would have talked. He would have been unable to control himself. He would have had to follow his natural inclination to talk and talk until he talked himself into a conviction. The puzzle of the country was that Hauptmann did not talk.

CHAPTER XI

WRITING IS NOT ALWAYS HANDWRITING

"WHAT shall I write?" has been a common question asked by my clients. For a long time I believed the question was asked because men and women believed seriously that *what* they wrote was important. Possibly they did but during more recent years it has been asked more as a start than for any other reason. Write anything. What you write does not matter. When you are analyzing the handwriting of your friends or strangers, it is not the words they write that counts or the writing instrument used that counts. Some will use pencils, some fountain pens, and others will prefer the straight steel pen. It does not matter. It is the strokes they make with the pen or pencil that count. But let me add here that some of my most interesting experiences have been with unusual writing instruments and out of the ordinary ways of writing. In each case, however, the writing strokes, and not how they were made, have counted in making exact analyses.

It has not always been so. Some very able graphologists of their time have had some extraordinary views on the subject. Even as late as twenty years ago a very able woman graphologist said that writing with red ink was a warning of danger. She probably believed what she said, but she was just as wrong as Don Felix de Salemanca, who in 1879 wrote in his book, *The Philosophy of Handwriting* that:

"Walt Whitman never writes decently when he uses that modern abomination—a steel pen. No one may hope to write a really good hand when using a metal stylus, for it emasculates every virile trait and completely obliterates its user's idiosyncrasies. Surely, 'The Good Gray Poet' can have no antipathy to a good grey goose quill which brings us so much nearer Mother Nature than does the forged metallic imitations. Whitman's chirography is not a pleasing or an intellectual one as a rule, although, at intervals, when guided by a flexible pen, it is not without a certain grandeur. His letters are frequently left unfinished; he discards the loops below the lines; words are contracted; a twist does service for the conjunction 'and'; erasures occasionally occur, and his manuscript is often hasty and heedless in the extreme. Then, his *d* is a rough kind of *delta* with a wide tailpiece that from its size, gives his writing the appearance of flourish from which abomination it is, however, perfectly free. Lord Bacon tells us 'there is not beauty but hath strangeness in its proportion'; and certainly, there is as much strangeness in the proportion of some of Walt's words as there is in some of his verse. Yet, for all these structures it must be confessed that far more vigor, real unaffected originality and even masculine beauty is discoverable in one short hasty note of Whitman's than in fifty folio pages of Bryant's or Whittier's conventional manuscript. Few of the chirographist's minor morals are neglected by the author of 'Leaves of Grass.' He is particular in his punctuation, careful to cross his *t*'s and dot his *i*'s and is quite *comme il faut* in his correspondence; in fact, shows that there is much method in his (presumed) madness. His signature is better executed than in the body of the letters and at times the Christian name is shortened to W."

There you have it, the explanation of a *graphologist!* In 1879, a man who wrote with a steel pen or stylus, who discarded an instrument "which brings us so much nearer Mother Nature"—the good grey goose quill—*failed to betray his personality,* because of his choice of a writing instrument!

Most certainly Don Felix would even now writhe in his grave if he faced this broad-stroked writing in this specimen which was not written with a pen at all, but still reveals intimately and fully the writer's complete nature. This unusual writing shows conclusively that the marks made by a writing instrument reveal the truth of how the writer thinks, acts, and wishes to act, no matter how odd the writing itself.

The man whose writing appears on the next page was introduced to me in the offices of a publishing house. Years before, the same building had been occupied by an opium den. Heavy Chinese carvings left by the previous tenants in their hurried leave-taking were still standing, looking down upon us. Graceful ladies carved from deep, dark wood stood in the corners, and sea serpents of the same dark wood curled around the ceiling. He was introduced as an editor, and three days later his handwriting was laid on my desk, along with a note saying plainly that the writer of the specimen considered grapho-analysis a fake, pure and simple.

It was a dare that had to be met, but after all it was easily met. The first thing to determine was that the writing was not pen, pencil, or crayon writing. That left brush writing, the kind the Chinese laundryman uses when he marks his parcels. Heavy brush strokes just like heavy pen strokes meant color—deep, rich hues, so much color that it became a vast reserve of the unknowable. The Orient alone provides such color, and the writing was Chinese brush writing. The small Greek *e's* repeated again and again, the breaks between the letters of the words emphasizing the literary tendencies of the *e's* revealed the

Here y'are, Brother Bunker—
a specimen of my so-called
"Chinese" writing!

Helen Keller

writer as a literary character. The great depth of color added to the literary evidence indicated mystery and the Orient. It was simple as adding two and two and making four. The picture of the writer was taking shape. The man who used the Chinese brush was or should be the writer of oriental mysteries. He was determined, very proud, and sometimes stubborn. He was practical in many ways, and persistent. This indicated that he was a prodigious worker, a writer who would turn out a vast amount of work. These were some of the details I worked out, and you will get others if you have followed closely the rules you have found in previous chapters. You will enjoy doing this. I did. Here was a man who did not believe his handwriting would reveal him, and still he had provided the key when he took his brush and wrote. It was thrilling, as you will find as you solve the mysteries of his personality.

I made my report, mailed it, and forgot it. When requests for handwriting analyses pile up you do not stop to remember one single specimen or writer. Handwriting never lies. I felt that Harry Stephen Keeler had revealed the truth as completely as though he had written with a pen. Later he was to admit that my report was correct, and I was to learn that when he submitted his writing he was already famous in England as a writer of mystery stories. Since then his books have come to America, adding to his reputation in mystery writing, and always he has mixed the Orient with the Occident, and always there are a maze of tangled threads, just as his writing indicated they would be.

In Chapter VII you will find the story of "Jeremy Evans," one of Mr. Keeler's characters, and the part that grapho-analysis played in creating that personality. It is sufficient now to recognize that Mr. Keeler's writing was handwriting, strange as it is. It is true he used a brush as a writing instrument, but he held the brush in his hand, which brings us down to the next illustration. Study this next specimen and ask yourself if it is or is not handwriting.

Surely it looks like handwriting. It has the far forward slant which you have found shows high emotional expression. It has the long final strokes which puzzled me in my school days when Prof. Dakin was urging me to drop the tails from my words. It has long loops, and *d's* that reveal sensitiveness, but it is not handwriting, even though it was written with a pen.

I did not make the report on this young lady's writing. One of my staff made it, and I knew nothing about it for a long time, but the writer's handwriting told the truth. That is the main thing. It showed the generosity, frankness, and desire to learn which you can find for yourself as you check over the page. The only thing that is different is the fact that Helene Wilmone Wilhelmi who wrote

Many thanks for my Grapho-Analysis. One would hardly believe that a simple little thing like handwriting, when read a certain way could reveal all of ones characteristics. Mine although not handwriting, because I hold the pen in my mouth, was a perfect reading" of my nature, even to the badness in me.

this letter saying her report was absolutely correct, was born without the use of either arms or legs, and this letter was written with the penstock held between her teeth. She did not use her hands because they were useless. She guided the pen with the movement of her head but her writing still told the truth.

When the doctors said she would never walk, the tiny girl became determined to walk. Today she uses her legs. They said she could not do many other things, but she does them. She finished high school, and today she operates a typewriter, plays and sings commendably, and has accomplished the almost impossible as an artist and dress designer. She has done all of these things by persistence and determination, both of which show plainly in her writing.

One thing in particular stands out in Miss Wilhelmi's writing. It is impulsiveness. She acts on the spur of the moment. Even a newspaper writer sensed this impulsiveness and wrote, "Miss Wilhelmi is far from the Pollyanna type of person. She probably is not even good Girl Scout material, for the things she does come impulsively, without any set plan or design and her interest in other cripples comes from her heart, and not from any motive to set herself up as an example and say 'Do as I do.' "

Her handwriting, though, for we may call it that for simplicity's sake even if it is not handwriting at all, shows the same care about details that would show in regular handwriting. It shows self-consciousness in the capital *M's* and the alert mentality of one who continually learns and desires to learn still more, expressed by the points on the *m's* and *n's*. It is all in the writing, even to her love of variety. Miss Wilhelmi likes change. This shows in her long lower loops. Further, she likes people, and shows this by the slant of her writing. Her widely spaced letters show her readiness to be generous, and the size of her loops show her lack of clannishness. Also, there is something more that is exceedingly interesting because it reveals what might have been. If Helene Wilhelmi had possessed an ordinary body she would have made a remarkable dancer. Her natural inclination for physical rhythm and graceful movement shows in her graceful *p's* in particular, and it is this appreciation of graceful movement and graceful lines that lies at the foundation of her artistic skill.

If you know of someone who is physically handicapped, show him Helene Wilhelmi's writing. Let him read this section of your book because by doing this you may be giving someone less fortunate than yourself a vision of that which he may make possible for himself.

For that matter, if you feel that you have not had as much of a chance as you would like, there is something in Miss Wilhelmi's writing to give you courage. She did not have a chance. She might have made just such an excuse, but she did not. She had persistence and pride. She wanted to do something worth while and she did it.

In exactly the same way Myron Angus, then a schoolboy in Canada, learned working toward the end that he would have a place in life. His teacher submitted Myron's writing for analysis.

Myron wrote it as part of an examination paper, but it is not handwriting any more than Miss Wilhelmi's letter is handwriting. Myron also holds his pen in his mouth. He did that when he wrote his examination. He did it when he took his drawing lessons, and when doing his other work. He is just like other men and women except that he holds his pen in his mouth because he cannot use his arms.

An interviewer found Myron Angus modest and if you will use your Emotional Expression chart you will discover for yourself that he has remarkable poise. He has a habit of doing each individual task carefully and exactly. He closes his *a*'s carefully, revealing that he neither talks too much nor boasts a great deal.

You will probably agree with me that it is a remarkable handwriting for a person who has no use of his hands, but as you study each stroke you will find that even as a boy he had ability. His broad-topped *m*'s and *n*'s and the *r*'s that are frequently half-squared across the top, all ex-

continents that touch the Atlantic are: North America, South America, Europe and Africa. The continents that touch the Pacific Ocean are: Asia, Australia, North America, South America. The continents that touch the Indian Ocean are: Africa, and Australia.

plain his creative ability and aptitude for drawing. The frequent thick spots of ink show his growing color sense, just as clearly as the extraordinary strokes made by the mystery novelist, Harry Stephen Keeler, give a picture of his remarkable sense of color and mystery. In the case of young Angus the color sense is not at all like Mr. Keeler's. It may never be, for they are entirely different personalities, but Myron Angus had a growing color sense, even when he was only a Junior Third Boy in his Canadian home school. He is constantly reaching out to develop new traits of character, and as he gains new mental habits they will show in his writing just as surely as your own writing will reveal your changes in character.

Both Helene Wilhelmi and Myron Angus have arms, but they are useless. The writer of the next letter does not have arms at all, but still he tells of his accomplishments, of how he rides a tricycle and plays football.

Bert Rouse wanted an analysis of his writing but his letter has never been answered because he did not give his address. I do not know where he lives, for he has not written me since. As you examine his handwriting you will see the reason. He asked me to examine his handwriting and so far as he can know, I was indifferent to his request. He would not ask again. Look at his tall *d's* and his short ones, and you see that he was too proud and too independent to ask a favor a second time.

Accordingly, the best I can do is analyze his writing here, just as I would if I were making it for him alone. Possibly he will see it and know that his request was not overlooked. This gives you, too, an opportunity to go along with me and work out your own report, using the rules you have learned.

His *i*'s are dotted carefully. The dots are round rather than dashes and circles. They are fairly close to the point of the letter strokes, so from the *i*'s alone you can be sure that Bert Rouse is loyal and careful. The fact that his writing is more vertical than slanted indicates his poise and supports the findings from the *i*-dots, that he is not scatterbrained.

His lower loop letters are not small, nor are they very large, so that you can be sure the lad is neither clannish, nor given to wild imagining. He writes his *t*-bars through the stem rather than over or above it, so you know he is practical. He will not dream about things that cannot be accomplished. He has *m*'s and *n*'s that are broad, showing that he reasons and does not act impulsively. This reasoning ability is shown again in the broad curves on the last half of the *h* when he makes that letter. Bert Rouse organizes or plans carefully, as shown by the well-balanced *f* with the loop above the line and the one below approximately the same length.

These, as well as many other traits, are here. They are

Oct. 12th., 1936

Dear Sir,—
I received your letter and was very glad
of it. I go to school and am now in grade - five
I am 13 years old I got my arms of when
I was seven. I started to school when
when I was nine. I can play foot ball and many
other games I can ride a tricycle. The other
boys ride bicycles But I manage it well
I have a sleigh dog and harness and dog
sleigh I can get time for $2.50 dollars. This
is all for now. and right soon
Yours truly
Bert Rouse

I wrote this with my mouth.

Bert Rouse, even though I have never seen him, and do not know where he is now. His writing reveals, however, that he is a real personality, and it is certain that he is telling the truth, because though his *a's* and *o's* are frequently closed, they are not deceitful strokes. Instead, these two letters merely reveal that this thirteen-year-old boy is more likely to keep things to himself than to talk freely. He is neither a whiner nor explainer, but possesses all of the poise and positiveness that a boy with arms might have.

It is meeting young folks like these that makes graphoanalysis so worth while. If there is anyone living who needs encouragement, such boys and girls need it, and when you understand the curlicues of handwriting so that you can properly evaluate them, you have a foundation for helping them see what life has to offer. They may be physically handicapped but they have keen minds, which are revealed as they write. With such an understanding it is easy to help those who need help, and who will profit by it.

Certainly Helene and Myron and Bert write interestingly. Even if they could use their arms they would be interesting young people, and for my part, I know that I have gained by analyzing their writing. Their courage is not that of words and protestations, but of facing great odds, recognizing them, and from the day of recognition on, thinking nothing more about them. For each of these young folks' life is out there, and they have no intention of letting it defeat them.

Of course you may say, "But they are young, and the older person who becomes handicapped has a more difficult road to travel." Possibly this is true. No one person can do more than argue this point, but it seems to me that Mr. Gawley, a Canadian who lost his arms after reaching maturity, gives the best possible answer.

Written by a steel Hand
Andrew A Gawley

Mr. Gawley lost both of his arms in a mill accident, yet his handwriting is firm and clear, and is accomplished by the use of steel hands, with which he grips the pen holder. The writing, however, will tell you more of Mr. Gawley's story because it reveals the engineering and scientific talent and inclinations which he had and which he put into use in conquering his problem. His handwriting even reveals his visionary nature by the way he used the crossbar on the *t* in *steel*. It is right at the tip of the letter, showing that he always sets his goal a long way ahead. It is almost the same in *Written* where the *t*-bar is not only crossed at the very tip of one of the letters, but is also long enough to show enthusiasm.

The *d* reveals pride, so great that though the young mill employee's father was blind and the injured man could have been a helpless cripple, he would not admit defeat. Those two men, each with a handicap that might have conquered other men, went about meeting their new problem. That was all there was to it. They were not complainers but doers, because they were proud. They set about making young Andrew a pair of steel hands. They were going to defeat their misfortune, and not be defeated by it. They made the hands, the same ones with which he chops wood; he uses the same steel fingers to tie his own shoe laces and even to thread a needle.

It is true that Andrew Gawley had mechanical talent. If you will study the signature of Charles P. Steinmetz, wizard of electricity, on page 57, you will find a marked resemblance in a number of their letters. They both possess poise, but they showed sympathy and understanding too, in these two specimens of writing. Mr. Gawley's writing reveals a more visionary nature, while the Steinmetz writing shows both his remarkable self-reliance revealed by the understroke for the signature, and his tenacity by the hook at the very end of the stroke. Neither shows a spirit of domineering, but both are steady, quiet, and orderly. It is in the *m's* and *n's* that their writing has the greatest similarity, and it is these two letters that reveal the scientific and creative natures of the men.

When you are tired and wearied by the problems of the day, I hope you will reread this chapter, for it may do for you what knowing these writers through their writing has done for me. They have shown me, as I have analyzed their writing, that handicaps are something to be faced rather casually, but overcome completely. You have certain handicaps. You may not see a way out, but if these men and women whose writing is not handwriting, but still writing, can overcome their handicaps and write as they do, you can win too. Andrew Gawley, mature, employed, might have grown discouraged, but he did not. He went on living, and the three young folks have done the same. They did not nurse their hurts. You cannot find one single stroke in their writing that indicates self-pity. They did not become supersensitive cripples, but made their lives normal.

These handwriting specimens, representing as they do so many interesting strokes, would easily be worth studying if they were handwriting, and as they are not, they become

doubly interesting. All of this in spite of what the graphology expert said about Walt Whitman's signature which I have included here because it is an interesting signature, and just as revealing as any other writing. When you have studied it you will know some interesting facts about that famous author, even if he did use a steel pen.

CHAPTER XII

JUVENILE WRITING POINTS THE WAY

WHEN you begin to analyze the writing of children and young people you will get a surprise; that is, it will be a surprise if you think the rising generation is all bad. If you wish to see good rather than bad in others, you will get considerable satisfaction.

Much is written about the younger generation. It is true many of them run helter-skelter, without regard to rhyme or reason, doing some of the most impossible things. They wreck motor cars and conventions, and all too often end up by wrecking themselves as well. All of this, though, is almost directly due to lack of family background. Usually the children themselves have great possibilities, but under a mistaken understanding of freedom or pure laziness, very many parents ignore their responsibilities either entirely or until it is too late.

When I say this I know very well I shall pull down upon my head parental criticism, but let me say here to those parents who disagree, your sons and daughters have come to me, they have written to me, and they are a pretty decent lot if you give them a chance. These young folks have written me letters asking how to correct weaknesses, and when they were sure I did not intend to be "holier than thou," they listened eagerly. In my staff I have hired boys who have stolen motor cars, and been in even more serious trouble. We have sat down together and analyzed their writing, discovered their good points, and their weaknesses, have weighed and evaluated them, and then tried to work out a plan of living that would use the good qualities. On the other hand, mothers and fathers have come to me saying that they did not know what to do with Bill or Tom or Mary, when a study of the parent's writing indicated that Bill could not be anything but a problem child if he reflected his father's nature.

Of course it is true that young people like to shock their elders. It is natural. A boy or girl growing up is trying out a thousand angles of living, and even the self-consciousness of some of them does not lessen their desire to attract your attention. Raising "whoopee" is, more of them have found, a good way to do it, and so, lacking family attention and understanding they get themselves and the self-righteous family into trouble. If the parents have money enough it does not make the front pages, otherwise it does.

Through it all, though, my experience of analyzing people, studying their motives, working with them in a sincere desire to help them, has convinced me beyond a measure of doubt that parents who have trouble at home should start studying their own handwriting and then study that of their children. The latter they will find amazingly encouraging, and their own specimens may give plenty of ground for immediate and detailed alibis.

If you are a father, and have a son who is puzzling you, thumb back through this book, and check your own writing. Study the boy's writing, and even if your findings embarrass you, take it like a soldier. Other fathers have done it, and you can too.

Mothers should do the same. Instead of talking about their problem sons and daughters they may frequently find the solution to their trouble by studying, first their own handwriting, and then the writing of the one who is causing the worry.

Grapho-analysis lays the blame where it belongs. You can prove this for yourself. Furthermore, most of the boys and girls who are getting started on the wrong path know it, and appreciate just criticism. Most of the problem girls and boys whose handwriting specimens have been submitted to me by worried parents show they are not bad but lack guidance.

On the other hand, brilliant children, those who have attracted great public favor, have not been merely talented children but they have had the benefit of training from parents who knew that the child represented a responsibility. An incident of this kind comes to mind as I write. On one of my many trips to Hollywood I met Baby Peggy Montgomery's father, and almost at once he asked me to analyze his young daughter's writing. Our meeting was in the studios of Nancy Smith, one of the most remarkable publicity women ever to settle in Hollywood, and the invitation came about as the result of an autographed lampshade that Miss Smith had in her private office. Using a fine grade of parchment, she had decorated the shade, or rather let her guests decorate it, with their signatures. Baby Peggy was among them, and Miss Smith asked me if it was possible to analyze the carefully drawn strokes necessary for writing on parchment. This is her writing.

Dear Mr. Bunker

I am Baby Peggy and ? am grown up, I would be very pleased to have you analyze my handwriting,
Yours Truly
Peggy Montgomery

The very first thing that attracted the eye was the little girl's ability to save, and I mentioned it. "You're right," her father said. "She even saves money out of her very small allowance. She loans it to her sister, but she collects, and then very likely she will turn around and buy something for her sister, but Peggy knows the value of money. Her mother and I agree on this, and I am glad it shows in her writing."

Peggy's writing revealed that she was not "just growing," but was being guided, and that the guidance started when she was a baby. Later when I received the more complete specimen reproduced here it was easy to follow out the effects of the careful training. You can check it just as I did. There is pride and integrity, the sort of pride that spurs the writer on to greater accomplishment rather than acting as a measure of self-satisfaction. There is care and frankness in the face of self-consciousness that might be made an excuse for failure. There is loyalty in the dotting of the *i's*, and growing determination in her downstrokes.

And, if you will recall for a moment the rules regarding musical talent you will find it in this writing. It is always so. If a boy or girl has talent it will show in the writing. If there is nothing more than aptitude for some particular kind of work, the pen strokes will reveal the tendencies. Take the writing of Raymond Baird for example:

In Regard to some of my experiences which you say might be of some interest to other boys I am sending you a short History of my

It is interesting as a specimen, and when you apply your grapho-analysis rules it becomes more so. You may have heard Raymond when he has appeared in your home-town theater or on a musical program, because for a long time he was the youngest saxophone artist before the public. However it is not my place to tell Raymond's story:

"When I was four and one-half years old," he wrote, "I went to a band concert at Salt Air Beach in Salt Lake City, and all through the concert I sat at mother's side beating time with my hands. After the concert the director, Mr. Owen Sweeten, came down and asked me if I would like to direct his band. Possibly he had seen me keeping time with the music. Of course I was surprised but I said I certainly would try. He took me in hand and after two or three months I directed his band. When I was five years old my mother took me to California where I began learning the saxophone under the tutorage of Professor A. B. Hunter, of Los Angeles; after about six weeks I played a solo at the concert in Los Angeles. Since then I have appeared in nearly every principal city in the United States.

"There are lots of people who think I am a sissy or something like that but I am not. I am a Boy Scout—second class—and soon will be first. I am just turned twelve years a short while ago, and the reason I can be a second class scout so early is because the scout officials in the town where I enrolled let me pass all my tests before I was of age.

"Now regarding my handwriting you may take any part of this letter for study, but I am afraid that you won't even be able to read my writing, much less find anything in it. Who knows. They say miracles never cease."

True enough, Raymond Baird had talent, and it was fortunate that that talent was outstanding enough to be cultivated. However, your boy or your girl may have talent, and unless that ability is discovered, may drift along aimlessly for years. Even if you think that you cannot get anything from handwriting, try it.

Use these rules on the handwriting of some boy or girl that you know and you may discover as much ability as I found in the signature of Dickie Moore, when he was one of the Hal Roach "Gang." A child in your neighborhood may

possess just as much of the practical as "Stymie" Matthew Beard as a child showed in his signature. You may discover

a Freddie Bartholomew next door, or a Shirley Temple just around the block.

All of this is possible, but far more important are the simple character traits that you can discover about the children in your own family. You may not have a Raymond Baird in your family, but you may have a boy who is learning to deceive you because he is copying you. You may have a girl who is afraid to trust you because you have made her afraid. It is in such simple truths that graphoanalysis offers you service, and if you are willing to apply these very simple rules you will be the gainer. In either case you can get the truth from handwriting.

CHAPTER XIII

FAMOUS HANDWRITINGS AND WHAT THEY TELL

ASIDE from aiding those who have needed honest guidance in matters of great personal importance, the choice of vocations, correction of weaknesses, or suggestions in matters of love, or family life, my greatest single satisfaction has been in knowing people. With grapho-analysis you do not merely meet them through introductions or mutual interests, but you come really to know them. You gain that knowledge of the individual which enables you to know how he or she will react under any given circumstance. This is truly knowing people, even though you may never meet face to face or converse with them across a luncheon table. What is more, they too may know you, and accordingly think of you as a friend rather than as a casual acquaintance.

This ability to fathom people, to understand them without depending upon hearsay gives you freedom, and for me it has made each new day interesting for what it might produce in the way of some striking personality, some unusual talent, or some strange combination of traits.

There have been so many cases of unexpected talents, where looking only at the external features would have made you hopeless about the individual's future; there have been so many interesting personalities that it has been completely worth while. Clothing, money, or the lack of it, environment, and training have not restricted my own findings of talent, nor the experience of discovering charm and integrity in strange places. All of this has been possible for me through grapho-analysis, and as you become more familiar with the rules and their application you will share in just such experiences.

As you go along analyzing handwritings with me or by yourself one simple truth must come to you. Rich and poor, high and low are much alike. When you have made this discovery for yourself you will have something that money cannot buy, nor fortune give you. You will have gained tolerance, which is needed in your life and in mine.

All of these thousands who have come to me for help have taught me this lesson so that looking back over these thirty years, I wonder if I have not learned more from those who have written me, than they have learned from me. I pass this very possibility on to you with the assurance that if you gain nothing else from grapho-analysis, you will still find yourself amply repaid for every hour you use in mastering these rules. You will understand people from the inside out rather than the outside in, and with this knowledge you will be qualified for the first time to judge others. You will also have gone far past the point where you want to judge, knowing that after all, judgment is not your right, knowing too that all the judgment in the world cannot be worth anything where facts alone are concerned, and that where you have facts such as you gain through grapho-analysis, judgment is not necessary.

In selecting these specimens from my scrapbook I have not made an effort to follow any set course. You have first the handwriting of my old friend Strickland Gillilan whose *Off agin, On agin, Gone agin, Finnigin* earned a permanent place for him in the field of American humorists.

You cannot miss Gillilan's musical sense, not if you have given any heed to the rule governing musical interpretation. He breaks his words time after time. In this clipping, for instance, there are only six words, but there are breaks between the letters of four of them, while there are three Greek *e*'s in two of the words, adding the literary complexion to the musical foundation of his nature. Strickland Gillilan became famous writing verse, but if you study this writing at all you will see that he simply had to write verse. It was as natural as breathing. He had talent and he used it, but he could not write intensely emotional verse because he is not an intensely emotional man. There is determination which is revealed by the downstroke of the *y*, and there is independence of thinking in the short-stemmed *d* which also shows sensitiveness. The *m's* and *n's* are made hurriedly, revealing a mentality that handles many details, clears them off, and is "gone agin" to some other task.

Summed up, even if you have never met Strickland Gillilan, or heard him speak, you still know him almost as well as you would if he were your neighbor. You know that he is not too fond of rich food, or of deep colors, and that he will be ruled by judgment rather than by an emotional storm. As you go along taking his writing apart, stroke by stroke, you learn to understand the man better.

Just as surely as Gillilan reveals himself as a poet, Knute Rockne, the famous football coach of Notre Dame,

revealed himself in his handwriting. During his life he was respected, admired by his men and by football fans wherever football fans live and have their being.

The strokes are simple, but they are strong from start

to finish. The *o* is open, indicating frankness, and the capital *R* is large as is the small *k*. There is unassuming self-reliance here, coupled with decisiveness. Knute Rockne knew what he wanted and expected to get it, not by being domineering, but by his ability to make decisions.

Someone in a Hollywood studio on one of my visits there mentioned Willy Pogany, the artist. "Will you take his handwriting home with you to your hotel, and make a report tonight?" my hostess asked. "I truly want to give him one of your reports and even though you are leaving tomorrow I wonder if you will do it." Naturally I did, for who would wish to refuse either a gracious lady or a great artist?

That night I made Willy Pogany's analysis, sitting in my hotel room, typing it out as I worked out the details. I saved the specimen from which I made that analysis, and because it is interesting, I have included it here for your study.

Take into consideration the sweeping enthusiam of the man, his marked aggressiveness shown by the way he makes the *p,* his vivid imagination, and his self-reliance. If you have never read the story of Pogany's life, you have missed an interesting document, but you still have a detailed picture of the man in these pen strokes. I remember I completed and mailed Pogany's report that evening because the next morning this note was in my hotel box:

"The rain that raineth ev'ry day
"Upon the Just and unjust feller.
"But more upon the just, because
"The unjust takes the just's Umbrella

Willy Pogany

"Being an artist I know how true it is that a person actually does express himself by the marks he makes with pencil or pen. I think you have done an excellent job on my writing and I thank you very much."

Such comments from a man so closely related to the use of pen strokes was as high praise as grapho-analysis could earn, but there have been hundreds, even thousands of them. One illustration of how grapho-analysis has perplexed people I am including here because it comes from a keenly intelligent woman.

This writer, Rosa Zagnoni Marinoni, is a popular club woman as well as author, with a wide experience in meeting and understanding people. You will find her *m's* and *n's* are like double *v's* wedge-shaped at the top, indicating a desire to learn, and wedge-shaped at the bottom, identifying the writing as one who analyzes that which she has learned.

Rosa Zagnoni Marinoni's writing was submitted to me originally by a magazine editor who wanted to publish a

story about her work, so that the report was made without her knowledge, from nothing more than a signature, and without any information on my part except that the editor wished to publish the story. Some time later her letter came to me through the offices of the magazine, an interesting instance of just how deeply grapho-analysis penetrates.

"The other day upon my return from a vacation in my old home town, New York," Mrs. Marinoni wrote, "I came upon a copy of the magazine in which you analyzed my handwriting. I read every word breathlessly, fearing to find what might have been a revelation to me of some hidden shortcomings. Your words at first startled me. You are too kind—and I said to myself, 'Is this I?' Then, on second thought I recognized that every word you wrote was the TRUTH. I gave the article to several friends and everyone said, 'This man knows you, for your own mother could not depict you more clearly.'"

Then, in her last paragraph Mrs. Marinoni brought out the most interesting part of her experience with the analysis.

"Yes, you are right in all you said, and to prove it I enclose an article which the *New York Telegram* ran this summer about me, in which, while giving forth my life, they mention all those qualities which you have written of me before this article ever came to light. There is this difference. The reporter had met me and had perused my work, while you never saw me, and I am sure knew very little (if anything) about me. So here is a toast to you, 'YOU ARE NO FAKE!' "

Of course I knew nothing about Mrs. Marinoni when I made her analysis. That is nothing but what her writing revealed. I have met possibly one in each ten thousand of the men and women, young and old, who have written me. Certainly not more than this number.

Writing from Paris, the famous author of the *Geography* that sold all the way around the world, sent me a full page taken as he said "from an indifferent article just finished." Then Frederick Willem Van Loon added, "I

don't remember what it was but it was written as I **write** and wish to God 'twere better."

Even if you do not have time for more than a cursory study of Frederick Willem Van Loon's writing you will notice the long and sharp pointed *m's* and *n's* indicating keen penetration and immediate comprehension. The *g's* are half-formed figure *8's* while the *a's* are like the *o's*, open, revealing the writer as a fluent user of words. Many words are broken, while you find the *i's* dotted with tiny dashes, a certain sign of mental annoyance. I remember that my analysis mentioning this trait brought the answer that grapho-analysis was the first means by which the writer's annoyance was properly placed. My study of his handwriting showed clearly that Mr. Van Loon was annoyed, all if not most of the time, because people would not think, but depended upon others to do their thinking for them.

The next specimen selected from my scrapbook is that of an American author who wrote one of the best international sellers, a religious novel, from which he never earned a cent. The story of how he overlooked a fortune

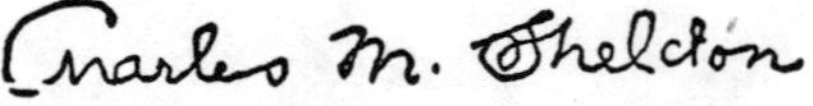

is a story in itself and entirely apart from the revelations of his handwriting. Rev. Charles M. Sheldon did, however, write the story *In His Steps,* which has been translated into many languages and published in many more editions. His writing gives you a clear picture of the man, and it explains incidentally how it was possible for Mr. Sheldon to have this experience and not become skeptical of people everywhere. You find the looped *s* here with a large lower loop indicating the man's imagination. Here too are the breaks between letters of the words indicating ability to catch the feel of music while showing poise and self-possession.

The whole temperament of this writing is to take justice and injustice impartially, meeting success and disappointment in the same way. Fame and wealth, or discouragement and disappointment are still the same to such a man whose emotional balance is such that he meets life from day to day without going down to defeat or becoming overbearing and self-inflated.

Ordinarily I do not ask people for their writing. They send it to me, but after I read *Vagabond House* I wanted to know the author. The best way to accomplish this was to ask for some of his writing. It is interesting as handwritings go.

Don Blanding's *g* shows literary inclinations, his long lower stem of the *g* showing unswerving determination while the capital *D* reveals his exclusiveness. Evidently he does not care for details for his *i* is not dotted, but let him tell about this part of his nature.

"It's curious," he said, "that details do irk me on everything except my drawing and my writing. On those two things I spend all of the patience that I have. If you notice the drawings in my latest books you'll see how detailed they are, but as for the rest I loathe all the fiddling and

fuddling that goes with most living processes. I'm mighty glad you enjoy *Vagabond House* so much. I truly enjoyed writing it and I like to have others enjoy it."

Which, after all, is that, and nothing more. If I had not enjoyed his verse I would not have come to know the man, with his independence of thinking. Because I now know Blanding as an individual, rather than as a poet, I find that I now enjoy even more than I did before the writing he has done. You will find it so, too.

If you were, for instance, an admirer of the late William Gillette of stage fame, his writing and what it revealed will interest you. Even before you read the words you will find evidence of keenest satire, and the underlying

We men — the few of us left — must stand by each other: that is the only way we can manage to exist a little longer. Trusting all to your Honor and Integrity — William Gillette —

depth of feeling that was second to the poise and emotional balance of the man.

It is a fine example of those traits as well as of the satirical qualities of his nature, but woeful would have been the result if those arrowheads had slanted downward. As it is, they were not, but think of what a domineering character would have existed if the crossbars on the *t's* had slanted downward. *If* this, and *if* that, but as you analyze more and more, in the endless range of specimens you will find you will cull out the "ifs" and deal only with what you see and know to be the truth. You will free yourself of petty prejudices, seeing people as they are, and not as you think they are.

It is even so in the case of Sally Rand, famous fan-dance girl whose arrests and publicity have spread across the country from coast to coast. Those who have denounced her and those who have praised her have provided plenty of publicity, but if I had expected to find anything serious in her writing I would have been disappointed. There is utter indifference to customs, enduring determination, and a high standard of personal integrity expressed by the tall *d*-stem in the signature. Every downstroke is a determined one, showing that having once set out upon a course of action the dancer will not turn back. This revelation from her handwriting brings us to a fact in regard to her life. Miss Rand set out to become a motion-

a whole page? Haven't
I been posed enough?
Must you know every
thing?

Sally Rand

picture actress, possibly a star. Her dancing has been a means to an end. It is part of the expression of determination. She started and she will not turn back, so without in any way attempting to forecast her future, it will be worth your while to see how she carries on toward her goal. Her handwriting shows that she will never retreat.

Is it by any chance unusual to turn the page of my scrapbook from the handwriting of Sally Rand to that of a great religious composer? If so, it is still the way they turn and I find the writing of the man whose *Every cloud will wear a rainbow* has been sung wherever religious songs are known. I have driven by rural churches on Sunday mornings in the cool of early summer, and have heard the words of the famous Rodeheaver hymn roll out through open windows, across meadows and wheat fields. I have heard it in churches where a trained choir led and great audiences followed, but it was not until Homer Rodeheaver asked for his analysis that I knew the man.

Here is his signature, taken from his letter telling me, "It is surprising what the handwriting does reveal," and saying that I had done a good job. Like so many others, he had not expected his writing to reveal him accurately, but it did. You will find warm emotional responsiveness in these few pen strokes. There is a deep appreciation of color and rhythm, too. The strong capital letters reveal self-reliance, and there is generosity in the finals. The *m* made sharp-pointed like inverted *v*'s shows the keen investigative brain of the composer.

The same desire to discover facts for herself was shown in the writing of the novelist, the late Gertrude Atherton. She said, "I am afraid my handwriting is too illegible for even you to make anything of," but her report went out just the same because no matter what kind of writing you have, you still have strokes, and you analyze strokes, not mere letter formations. This is interesting writing, especially if you recall your various rules and apply them. You do not need to read the words. You have the strokes of Mrs. Atherton's pen, and that is all you need. These strokes convey the enthusiasm that swept others along in the faith of this great writer. They reveal warm and expressive emotions, with a visionary desire for accomplishment that was backed up by the will to make those visionary hopes come true. The frankness, kindliness and self-reliance, all coupled together with a highly impulsive friendliness, gave Mrs. Atherton that intangible something called charm.

This specimen which the late Richard Le Gallienne sent me from France has been reproduced the exact size of the original. Like Rafael Sabatini, Le Gallienne's writing was small, revealing remarkable concentration. There was a strong strain of musical interpretation, or understanding of music, which translated into words meant a keen sense of word selection. The heavy strokes showed not only depth of feeling but also color sense, emphasizing the care and discrimination the writer used in selecting the words he wanted to convey his meaning. The figure 8 for the g's restricts the working of the music and color influences to literary lines, so that no matter if you had never heard of the man you might still know he wrote as a poet writes and felt as a poet feels.

There is no need for me to go along with you on this analysis because you can make it for yourself. It is all written here, while in the previous chapters you have had the keys with which to unlock each of the mysterious strokes, not only in Le Gallienne's writing but in the writing of every other specimen in this book. For that matter, these same rules make it possible for you to know yourself as you have not done before. You may study your friends, and doing this, have an honest understanding of their efforts, their ambitions, and their purposes. Those who have seemed to be one thing you may find as entirely different personalities. You have friends whom you have

The presence that rose thus so strangely beside the waters, is expressive of what in the ways of a thousand years men had come to desire. Hers is the head upon which all "the ends of the world are come", and the eyelids are a little weary. It is a beauty wrought out from within upon the flesh, the deposit, little cell by cell, of strange thoughts and fantastic reveries and exquisite passions.

Walter Pater: "The Renaissance."

misjudged. All people have such friends, but when you grapho-analyze them you honestly get acquainted, and as a result you will find yourself altering opinions of long standing.

If you have analyzed these writings as you have come to them in the book, you have gained something. I did. These men and women have given us a chance to look at greatness, and to understand it, for each of these writers is in his or her own way, among the great.

Also they have done something more. Knowing the great we now have the key to the simple truth that each person has within himself something of the great. *You* have that something, just as others have it, so that no matter what comes, if you build with what you have, there is something in life for you. The great are not without weaknesses any more than you or I. They have emphasized their character assets, and have ignored the weaknesses which might have grown into great handicaps. Those who have achieved a place in the world have not spent their days and nights in self-pity because of weaknesses. Instead, both individually and collectively, they have made places for themselves by driving toward a goal, just as you can do.

CHAPTER XIV

CRIMINALS REVEAL THEIR TRUE NATURES

IF Asta Eicher, living in the suburbs of Chicago had known even the simplest rules of grapho-analysis, and had used them in sizing up the writing of her strange correspondents, she and her three children might have lived. Instead they died, victims of a mass murderer, even though that murderer advertised his deception and cruelty in the love letters he wrote the widow, promising her comfort, and happiness, and a father's care for the three orphans. Every line of his writing revealed selfishness and cruelty. Indeed it was such a vicious nature that one of my assistants glancing at the writing as it lay on my desk, recognized the warning signs in the love letter which was sent to us for examination after the crimes were committed.

For many years it has been my habit to be at my office by seven o'clock in the morning so that the first mail of the day comes directly to my desk. On this particular morning I opened a registered letter from Clarksburg, West Virginia, merely glanced at it, and laid it aside for further study. Later, one of my assistants came into the room and standing half the distance of the room gasped out her amazement and disgust. "What a terrible character," she said. She was correct. It was a terrible character that stared up from the paper, although when we read the words the letter became exceedingly kind and considerate. It simply did not seem possible that any man could be so degenerate, but his writing told the truth. Our recognition of his character came too late to save either the Eicher family or Dorothy Lemke of New England, who died and was buried in the same grave with them.

If Asta Eicher had only known something about grapho-analysis! But she did not know anything about it. Possibly if she had she would have memorized the simple rules that could have saved her life, and the lives of her children. No one knows. Only one thing stands out in all of the mass of details that have been published and re-published in the newspapers and in magazines. Asta Eicher was left a widow with a small amount of property. She grew lonely, and, feeling the responsibility of caring for three children, enrolled in a correspondence club. Possibly it would be just as well to call it what it was, a matrimonial bureau.

It was then that Harry Powers, living in a West Virginia city, read the advertisement. Using the name of Connie Pierson, he wrote a glowing letter, telling in detail about his wealth, his loneliness, and longing for love. The letter was filled with sweetness, if you could not read the nature of the man in his handwriting. His writing revealed him in his first letter for just what he was, a degenerate, a liar, sensual, greedy, and cruel.

Asta Eicher read the thrilling promises of love and protection, and because they were the thing she wanted to hear and believe, she accepted them as true. She read the words and not the pen strokes. One letter followed another, until the widow Eicher promised to become Mrs. Pierson. The widow thought she was getting security, and a home for her children, while Powers knew he had caught another believer who had some property which he wanted for himself.

He was a gross deceiver as you can discover for yourself by checking the chart which I have made from a few lines of his writing. These lines running from different letters to A and B show clearly just how strong the evidence of deception was against him in his own writing. Follow the four lines leading from B. Each ends in an *a* that starts with a hook. In *care* the *a* is open at the top while in *may* it is so badly blurred that there is no opening although it would be there if the writing had not been so badly blotted. The capital *A* in *Again* is hooked and open-mouthed. In *have* the *a* is barely closed. In four *a*'s three are open, wide open, indicating talkativeness, while the initial hooks show deceit. The other lines leading from *A* extend to open-mouthed *a*'s and the *g* made with the first part like an *a* is the same. All of these *a*'s spell deception and talkativeness, a character that merely talks because talk is cheap, and deceives because it is easy for him

B

*Wont you write to m
you may care to ask
best of my ability can
tell me will be const
I have a small photo
yours would be of us
Again, — Please*

A

to talk, and because his natural inclination is toward deception.

Asta Eicher might have seen all of this; she might have been protected by being forewarned, but she did not know how to read the handwriting signs that Powers put into his writing. He did not know that his writing revealed his greed and falseness or he would never have written the letters.

It was ignorance all the way around, while you, if you will keep these two rules in mind, will have protection. There is no deviation from them, no exceptions. When you find writing that is filled with *a's* like those in Power's writing you may look for trouble, treachery, deceit, coupled with a grasping nature that will not stop at anything. Powers did not. Not even murder. But every line of his letters was to rise up and damn him later. Not alone for his deception, but for the sensuality of his nature.

Whenever you find a page of handwriting that is blotted, blurred, and muddy, look for the sensualist, the beast, the sex-mad writer. It is not heavy writing that reveals the sensuality, but the blots and blurs. Heavy writing means depth of feeling, color sense, sensuousness, but not sensuality. It is the writer who blots and smears what he writes, who puts the mark of the beast upon himself, and, just as in the case of the deception and talkativeness, there are no exceptions.

Furthermore, all sex criminals are not master deceivers as was "Connie Pierson" Powers. Others yield to desire, either impulsively or coldly and selfishly. Take the blots and smudges in the specimen. The very first glance shows that the writer is extremely responsive to emotions. He is impulsive; therefore, his actions indicate a lack of planning. The blots and ink smears give him away though, so that there is no mistaking the sex desires that drive him on. These blots and smears always reveal sensuality.

Paul Kauffman was another of the sex-mad killers, utterly selfish, interested in satisfaction of his desires, and willing to go to any ends to gain it.

The Paul Kauffman case came to me by way of a song, and was probably one of the strangest criminal cases ever brought to me by an attorney. Young Kauffman had been arrested for running fake advertising offering employment to country girls. According to the police, Kauffman advertised for a companion for his little girl, and expressed a preference for country girls. He would receive the answers, correspond with the girl, explaining the remarkable opportunity offered by the job, and arrange to meet the young woman on her arrival in the city. He would fulfill his part to the letter, meeting his prey, taking her to dinner, and then making insistent advances. His advertisement was run repeatedly and no one will ever know how many girls were attracted by it. Finally, however, a young woman with more than ordinary courage reported him to the police and he was picked up for questioning. He pleaded guilty immediately, and was given a jail sentence. While all of this was going on, the homicide squad was

second floor, in 3 West". Lloyd has
the Key cell on Four, and Mike
and Frank are right next to me
Closing as per Instruction
Hoping to hear from you soon
and regular. Best, and sincerest
regards to you, your family and all
you Love. Remember me always as
a Friend and Buddie
Paul H. Kauffman.

investigating the brutal slaying of a young woman in one of the city parks.

Under ordinary circumstances, Kauffman would have been safe, but in this instance coincidence played a part, and he was accused of the murder. It was while he was awaiting trial that his attorney came to me with a specimen of the young man's writing and a copy of a song poem the prisoner had composed. The idea back of this visit was not to get an ordinary grapho-analysis of the prisoner's writing, but to discover if possible that the young man had a great but undeveloped talent for music, possibly that he was a genius, and to use that fact if discovered as part of the plea at the trial.

There was nothing to do but to explain to my visitor that I could not discover that which did not exist, and accordingly would not show in the handwriting. Also, that if I did find such talent, I would include this fact in my analysis, just as I would identify every other character trait or inclination discovered in the writing.

We agreed on this, and when I was alone I prepared the analysis. Paul Kauffman did not have musical ability. He lacked rhythm, and was utterly lacking in interpretation, but he did have a vivid imagination expressed by his large *y* and *g* loops. He had a remarkable readiness to talk as shown by the wide open *a* and in the letter *g*. Also, he was ruled by self-interest and by sex. The blots that started in the first line of his writing were repeated time and again. It was not the pen nor the paper, but the nature of the writer cropping out. Every line had letters that should have been open, but were closed with ink. His *e's* were merely black circles; his *a's* were almost always closed, and muddy spots were scattered over the page. There was no denying it.

According to these findings the report was prepared and submitted, and with it I mailed a confidential letter to the attorney, telling him my detailed findings, pointing out that even if Paul Kauffman were freed he would be a potential sex criminal; that no matter where he was or how he lived he would still be so sensual that his desires would rule and wreck his life.

Writing may be very heavy. The full page of Harry Stephen Keeler's writing made with a brush, which you have in another chapter, is extremely heavy, but it is not muddy. It is the blotted, smeared writing that spells *Danger*. Watch such a writer and do not permit yourself to trust him no matter how much he promises. This holds good no matter what position the writer may hold. It is true regardless of whether the writer is a man or woman, young or old. Paul Kauffman was younger than Harry Powers, but they both killed as a result of their abnormal sex desires.

Of course all sex cases do not end in murder. One of these which came to me early in my grapho-analysis research did not end in murder, but it did end in disgrace. A very popular minister, associated with an equally popular church, submitted his writing. It was grossly sensual. Blotted, blurred, muddy, from start to finish, there was only one thing to do. The writing showed he was sensual and I put it into the report, and sent it out promptly. Almost immediately I received a scathing letter, damning grapho-analysis, denouncing my own work and threatening dire punishment. I filed the letter and waited. Years went by, and then the home city of the very popular young minister woke up to find his name in scare headlines. The young minister was charged with being a "come on" member of the white slave traffic. Charges were dropped and he disappeared, but years before, his writing had revealed his character. The newspaper story was news to others, but his handwriting had revealed his true nature.

It would be easy to go on and on, recalling one case after another, but lust and murder are not pleasant to recall, and these circumstances provide sufficient illustration of the handwriting peculiarities that show dangerous sex characters. This rule about muddy writing never fails. It was in the writing of Winnie Ruth Judd, slayer of Agnes Anne LeRoi and Hedvig Samuelson in Phoenix, Arizona.

It was in the handwriting of Edward Hickman, youthful slayer of Marion Parker in Los Angeles, and it is always in the handwriting of sex criminals.

Further, these murderers wrote muddy hands, not only at the time or about the time they committed their crimes, but months before, so that if anyone familiar with the laws of grapho-analysis had examined the writing of even a single one of them, the *Danger* sign would have been recognized immediately, and lives possibly saved.

If I emphasize this warning it is because men and women are so much inclined to look on the outside at what seems to be, to listen to glowing promises they want to hear and accept the false as the good. It is not necessary in dealing with either friends or strangers to doubt them. You do not need to go through life cynically unwilling to believe in the goodness and decency of people. Not at all. In fact if you will remember these few simple rules, and will apply them along with the others given in various chapters you will find yourself making more and better friends. You will understand people and be fairer in your judgments. You will be more inclined to judge yourself fairly, see your own weaknesses and strong points, and so be better equipped to get along with others. All people are not bad and there are no perfect ones. Only a few people are really bad, and even the bad ones have some good that you can find if you can analyze handwriting. Even these sensual murderers showed some very fine qualities. They possessed certain traits of character which they needed to understand for themselves, but they had no one to show them what the sensuality and sex longings that burned within them would produce.

Instead of being acquainted with themselves they stumbled along through life and eventually committed crimes. Say what you will, these crimes were as much the lack of understanding as they were of lust. No one of these convicted creatures understood himself. Not even one of them knew he was rushing to disaster, because of lack of knowledge. This is a condition that contributes to crime. Boys and girls grow into maturity without self-understanding. They succeed or they fail, blame or get blamed for events that occur, but all without understanding. Out of this complicated situation criminals are born and developed. They do not know themselves and they do not understand those around them, so stumble or drift through life with more chance of failure than success. Grapho-analysis is one of the things that could help solve this problem. It provides a fair, unbiased estimate of others, and of oneself, which is not lack of justice or friendliness but rather the fulfillment of both virtues in the highest degree.

There has been scarcely a week during my years of handwriting research when I have not examined at least two or three specimens of developing criminals. Thousands of young men and women, as well as older ones, have asked for analyses of friends whom they have trusted, and in many cases getting the exact truth has saved unhappiness, misery, and possibly bloodshed. There have been women who have insisted that the analyses of lovers were all wrong, but who have come to me later thanking me for the truth. You will have such experiences when you have mastered these rules sufficiently to put them into practical use. What is more, you will find that, without being meddlesome or out of place, you are doing things for people. When you reach this point you will see the real service you can render humanity by applying these principles.

Even as I write this I dare to urge you once more to master these rules that identify the sex criminal. He is a growing menace and every bit of help you can give in correcting the condition will be just that much help to your race and country. In addition you will be directly increasing the safety of those who are dear to you, for the sex criminal is dangerous and may be found in any locality or environment.

CHAPTER XV

QUESTIONS AND ANSWERS

My experience in training grapho-analysts scattered all over the civilized world justifies this final chapter. My students have always asked many questions about points of instruction they have covered. There is so much to grapho-analysis, while at the same time it is so easy and so simple to apply, that many of those who study it fail to get many of the essentials at first. You may share in this, so you will not find these questions and answers out of place.

Grapho-analysis deals with such a constantly changing scene, each individual different from all others, that it never loses its fascination, but in spite of this, it is a very great subject. Even when studied seriously over a period of many months there are always new truths to uncover, so even after reading the chapters that have gone before, you will find this one of great help. The questions for this section are arranged with the idea of giving the greatest possible range of explanation while the alphabetical arrangement will add to the convenience in locating the rule applying to the trait of character about which the question has been asked.

A

Ques. 1—How is *aggressiveness* shown?

Ans.—By a sharp forward stroke instead of a loop for *g*, *y*, and *j*. This rule also includes the letter *p*.

C

Ques. 2—What does it mean when a writer slants some letters far forward, others less so, some backward, and some almost vertical?

Ans.—It means exactly what the writing indicates. The writer is *changeable*. You know that forward slanting writing shows emotional expression, that vertical or back-hand indicates absence of emotional expression. When you find writing at various slants, or angles, you may be absolutely sure that the writer is expressive on some occasions, and on others the same or similar circumstances will not arouse any show of feeling.

Ques. 3—What is the meaning of letters that break at the base line of writing?

Ans.—When *a*, *o*, *d* and *g* are broken in the circle at the base line of writing, it is an unfailing sign of a dangerous or *criminal* character. This is true no matter how innocent such a writer may seem to be.

Ques. 4—What is indicated by very small circles instead of loops for *g*, *y*, and *j*?

Ans.—Such writers will be inclined to make few close

or trusted friends. They may be good mixers, but at heart they are *clannish* in the sense that they allow few intimates.

Ques. 5—What is the meaning of small writing?

Ans.—The smaller the writing the greater the *concentration* of the writer. There are no exceptions.

Ques. 6—When *m's* and *n's* are made sharp-pointed like *w,* what trait is indicated?

Ans.—Sharp or needle-pointed *m's* and *n's* show keen *comprehension.* Such writers will meet another for the first time, and know without analysis or reasoning what they think of the stranger. They learn easily when they apply themselves, but rarely analyze that which they have learned. When they do analyze, you will find that they make frequent v-shaped joinings at the base line of writing.

Ques. 7—What is indicated when *t's* are not crossed in any way, and when the dot is omitted in the *i?*

Ans.—Such writers are *careless* about details. They may be sincere, capable, but such a writer will be given to *carelessness,* especially about small matters.

D

Ques. 8—What is shown by the downstrokes of *y, g,* and *j?*

Ans.—When the strokes are straight, they indicate *de-*

termination, the degree of the *determination* shown by the thickness or heaviness of the stroke. The longer the downstroke, the greater the *determination.*

Ques. 9—How is *diplomacy* revealed by handwriting?

Ans.—When the letters in a word retain their clear formation, but grow smaller as they near the finish of the word.

E

Ques. 10—How is *enthusiasm* shown?

Ans.—Long, sweeping *t*-bars, above or across the *t*-stem show *enthusiasm.* High emotional expression is frequently mistaken for *enthusiasm,* but it is not considered as such in analyzing handwriting. On the other hand, unexpressive natures are rarely *enthusiastic.*

G

Ques. 11—How is *generosity* revealed?

Ans.—True *generosity* is shown by long final strokes on words. Many times impulsive people seem to be generous because they act without thinking, give without deliberation, and later regret their offers of kindness.

H

Ques. 12—What stroke or strokes indicate a sense of *humor?*

Ans.—There is a difference between wit and a sense of

humor. The latter is shown by wavelike flourishes before letters, usually the capitals, *M, N,* and *W,* but may also occur before the small letters of this group.

I

Ques. 13—What does it mean when a writer dots the *i's* with circles?

Ans.—The result of extended tests shows that such writers like to do things, anything they do at all, in a manner somewhat different from the way that others do it. They like to affect distinctions in their acts and interests. In the writing of an ignorant person these circles reveal ostentation, but no matter where you find it, the circle for the dot is evidence of *individuality.*

Ques. 14—Do the loops of the *h* and *k* have any value or meaning?

Ans.—Yes. When very much enlarged in proportion to the other strokes, they indicate a vivid *imagination* along spiritual or visionary lines.

Ques. 15—What is the meaning of frequent breaks between letters of a word?

Ans.—Breaks *between* letters are entirely different from broken letters. When you find frequent breaks between letters in the body of words of a written page you may be sure the writer is *intuitive* or possesses that appreciation of music that is highly important to the proper interpretation of music. Many times such writers do not play musical instruments but will admit deep love for music. They will also admit that they play hunches or sense that which is about to occur. Breaks between letters in the body of a word do not mean that the writer plays a musical instrument, and in many cases the writing of very accomplished technical musicians does not show such breaks. In those cases where the breaks do not occur you will find that the creditable musical performance is due to technique and emotional expression, combined possibly with a high sense of tone values. The breaks themselves indicate the *psychic,* or *intuitive* sense.

J

Ques. 16—How is *judgment* indicated?

Ans.—Vertical writing indicates lack of emotional influence in regard to actions or decisions.

L

Ques. 17—What is the meaning when *i's* are dotted with small round dots?

Ans.—Such dots indicate *loyalty*.

O

Ques. 18—What does it mean when the line of writing slants upward?

Ans.—*Optimism*. Such writers cheerfully expect that everything will turn out for the best.

P

Ques. 19—What is revealed when the writing line slants downward?

Ans.—The line of writing slanted downward shows *pessimism*. Such a writer is matter-of-fact, lacks cheerfulness. When the slant is very pronounced it is a sign of fatalism.

Ques. 20—When the *t*-bar is written back of the *t*-stem, what is the meaning?

Ans.—It shows varying degrees of *procrastination,* depending upon the number of times it is repeated as against the number of bars that actually cross the stem. Sometimes you will find that a writer scarcely ever crosses the stem of the *t,* but this is not common. One who fails to cross the stem half of the time and who writes the bar back of the stem is a confirmed procrastinator.

S

Ques. 21—What does an arrowlike crossing for the *t* indicate?

Ans.—Keen *sarcasm* if written directly from left to right. When written to the right and downward it indicates a domineering nature.

T

Ques. 22—What is the sign of *talkativeness?*

Ans.—Wide, open-mouthed *a's* and *o's*. As the small *g* is made up of an *a* with a loop, the same rule applies to open-mouthed *g's*.

W

Ques. 23—How is *will power* indicated?

Ans.—By crossbars of the *t*. The bar may be long, or short, because the length of the bar does not reveal the will power. It is the thickness of the bar that is important. The thicker the bar or stroke, the stronger the will power.

Ques. 24—Is it possible to analyze handwriting in a foreign language?

Ans.—There is only one answer. If your home is in the United States or Canada, you are a foreigner to a German, Italian, Chinese, or Scandinavian. Your writing, though, can be analyzed, and this is true of any language except the oriental stroke writing. Even this may be analyzed, although it has not been worked out in such detail as have other stroke combinations. You can analyze foreign writing, because such writing is made up of strokes, and it is the stroke values that count.